# A CASUAL COMMENTARY

# A CASUAL COMMENTARY

BY

ROSE MACAULAY

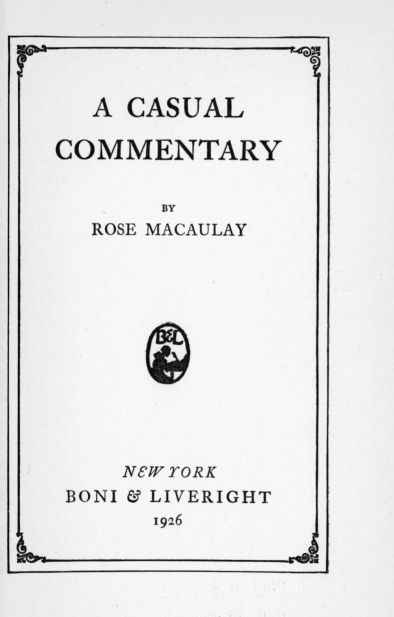

*NEW YORK*
BONI & LIVERIGHT
1926

# CONTENTS

# NEW YEARS

# A CASUAL COMMENTARY

## NEW YEARS

HERE, then, we are—arrived at another spin of the wheel. Another January; another New Year; presently another quickening of the sap in the trees, of green in the undergrowth, of the blood in man's veins, of activity among publishers and birds; in brief, another year.

The chief food for thought offered by this reflective period is, how strangely infinite in variety are years! How many millions of them has man now suffered or enjoyed, or both, since he first began to suffer and enjoy at all; and yet each of these millions has borne to him how different a face! And not to man alone, but to birds, beasts, and vegetation. "The holly is red this year," we say; or "The spring is backward"; or "The summer is wet and cold." We possibly exaggerate these natural differences, and very likely (in these islands at least) the holly is red, the spring backward, and the summer wet and cold, every year. But small differences there perceptibly are. And in the human world, in the occurrences which beset, all the world over, mankind, how many and how great distinctions appear! One year throws up war, another peace, another revolutions, general elections, and Wembley; and we may be sure that every future year will do its part and produce some new and intriguing feature, both in the world at large and in the private lives of each of us.

For no year is like another, except in this—that all are remarkable for important and exciting events. An important time : that is what the times we live in have always been. Read any newspaper, be it never so far back, never so recent, and you will find the same new year's comments. "A momentous period is just closed," or "is now proceeding," or "is about to begin." See that admirable chronicle of wasted time, the *Annual Register,* which has for two centuries recorded, at the end of each year of history, its outstanding events. "Last year," it said, commenting on 1801, "was fraught with a greater number of important events than any other which has elapsed since the commencement of the *Annual Register."* Was it? Or did the events only seem so very important because so near? "The great and extraordinary affairs of war, politics, and revolution," comments the surprised *Register* of an earlier year, "which have agitated almost every part of life." Extraordinary? Or would not "usual" be a more apt word? For January 4th, 1762, we have the bored and *blasé* statement—"War was proclaimed against Spain, at the usual places, with the usual solemnities." That reads more accurately.

What a tendency is this in us to regard as extraordinary the normal functionings of life on this our apparently quite ordinary planet. What strange, imagined norm is this that we have so unaccountably conceived and set up in our minds as a standard of comparison, thereby admiring as extraordinary the ordinary doings of humanity? Memorable times; a memorable world; no doubt a memorable race. Possibly, even, an important race. . . .

"In history for various reasons the closing year stands remarkable," comment the newspapers at this last year's end, as, indeed, they have always commented, and as men doubtless commented one to another in all the æons before newspapers were. Not only in those years which have survived the swirling waters of oblivion and seem to us memorable even now as we look back; not only in years of wars and conquests, great floods and earthquakes, prodigious discoveries; but in each one of those placid, obscure, unostentatious years, now sunk and drowned long since in time. Not only years when, to quote the *Register* for 1762, "the flames of war threatened to spread in every part of Europe," and "if we look to southward the clouds are gathering there also," but those serener years when such minor incidents were recorded as that a comet was discovered by Mr. Dunn at his academy in Chelsea, and Vesuvius erupted, and Lord Ferrers was killed in the Strand, and official relations with the Porte were suspended because a missionary in Turkey was discovered with disrespectful reflections on the Turkish religion in his carpet bag. Not merely the year 1000 which was to end the world and introduce the millennium, but those years which rather flatly followed this; even these, we may be sure, were not dismissed as trivial, but firmly recorded as "these momentous times" by those who had thought ere then to have seen all times shrivelled to naught in the fiery thunderbolts of eternity. How rich in incident and momentum, "agitating," as the *Register* has it, "almost every part of life," must have been every year lived by the early inhabitants of these islands, confronted always with what the press of to-day describes as "acute cases of human and national antagonism, which persist in spite of the plain warning that their continuance will wreck civilisation." Yes, indeed. Britons, Romans, Saxons, Danes, Normans, Spaniards, theologians, Germans, French, Egyptians, Asiatics, Russians, Turks, politicians, writers, and motorists, all acutely annoying each other in turn, all engaged from the first times even down unto these last in wrecking civilisation—which is, therefore, as we now see it.

An infinite variety in sameness indeed. Life is prodigious, and so is each one of its years. A long revue, with one remarkable turn succeeding another, until the curtain shall fall. We wait between the turns like children, agape for whatever may arrive. We may like it or not when it comes; but it will, at the least, be exciting. *Temporum varietates;* as Cicero said, how amusing these are! And, if not so startlingly new after all, we imagine them to be so, which comes to the same thing.

# SOME SPECULATIONS ON HUMAN CREATURES

# HOW TO CHOOSE A RELIGION

HOW to choose a religion. How comparatively seldom this problem seems to be discussed. Inquiries and helpful words on how to choose a profession are bandied continually about. How, even, to choose a husband or a wife, and at what age to do so, is a point frequently discussed in our less scholarly press. How to become a journalist, a novelist, a poet, or a member of parliament; how to choose a political party, a style in hair-dressing, a tooth-paste, a dinner, or a hat—on all these are our journals glibly and brightly eloquent. But on how to choose a religion— a theme perhaps too weighty for them—they maintain a conspiracy of silence.

Not so will I. For it is, surely, even more important to have the right religion than the right tooth-paste. I do not mean by the right religion, as Mr. Belloc says he does, the *true* religion, for truth is too dim a figure at the bottom of her well to be drawn up by any casual explorer; neither should we know her if we saw her; and, if you come to that, what is truth? No; the right religion for each person is the religion best fitted to his particular needs and capacities.

There are many ways of selecting a religion. Some people scarcely select, but merely retain that, if anything, which was imparted to them in youth. For such undiscriminating and conservative souls the problem does not arise. Many others do not choose a religion, but choose not to have one; for these too the religious problem is reduced to simplicity. But I am considering the vast body of those who do desire a religion, but do not quite know what form they would prefer. For such there are several good methods of selection. One is to spend your life in travel, research, and inquiry, until all the varieties of religious experience are known to you, and then, at an advanced age, to select that which appears to you to be preferable. If means and time do not permit of travel, the works of Sir J. G. Frazer should be carefully perused, together with all the Greek and Teutonic philosophers, the Hebrew Scriptures, and many modern American books on various forms of credulity. But Salt Lake City should be visited in person, as most of the literature on the religion of this town is, one way or another, a little biassed.

The drawback to this laborious method is that it demands not only a lifetime of study, but a brain qualified to apprehend, balance, and judge, and how few brains are this! Most of us prefer and are better fitted for a less deliberate and a more impulsive method.

I have heard it said (but, fortunately, it is not true), "By their hymns you shall know them." Those who believe this will no doubt be moved to study the hymn-books of the various religions under consideration. It is not really a fair test, for a religion's hymns are often the religion at its least intelligent; but still, having seen the hymns, you have at least the satisfaction of knowing the worst. The hymns of most so-called savage tribes have a certain monotony, both of words and tune. They often run something like this: "Oh, Boo-Boo" (or whatever the deity's name may be), "to placate you we offer you this victim slain by the knife. Descend, therefore, and eat, and spare the rest of us this time." That is the sort of thing. It is chanted very loudly, to the accompaniment of tom-toms and of what are known as nameless orgies. But it is probably quite unfair to judge the religions of our black brethren by their hymns. When they embrace Christianity, they usually become evangelical, and their hymns are rather worse than before, but have catchy tunes.

Neither is it kind or just to judge the Protestant sects by the hymn-books of Messrs. Moody and Sankey. For instance, one of these hymns begins, "I should like to die, said Willie, If my papa could die too; But he says he isn't ready, 'Cause he has so much to do"; and another, "Well, wife, I've found the model church, And worshipped there to-day." The hymns in the Ethical Church hymn-book have more balance, and say, "We must strive by education Man's condition to improve." They also cry, more emotionally, "Nearer, mankind, to thee."

But, leaving hymns and liturgies aside, let us consider particular churches, their qualities and habits. If it is, say, the Christian religion we are contemplating and wish to adopt, it will take us some time to decide which branch to join, for its varieties are almost in-

numerable.  To mention a few of the more prominent,
we may, for instance, be Roman Catholic, Orthodox,
Anglican, Quaker, Presbyterian, Calvinist, Wesleyan,
Baptist, Congregationalist, or Plymouth Brother.  Of
these the Roman Catholic branch has dignity, antiquity,
and authority, and will save you a lot of trouble in
deciding for yourself what to believe, for it knows the
truth and tells you.  Many people like this.  On the
other hand, marriage with non-Catholics and divorce
with anyone at all are troublesome in this Church, and
a good deal of attendance at services is expected.  The
Orthodox branch also has dignity and an ancient tradition, but its clergy do not always look what our novelists call well-groomed.  Many of them do up their hair
with hair-pins.  They are not allowed to worship
statues, but only eikons, or images in bas-relief.  The
Orthodox mind sees a distinction here that no other
Church has yet grasped.  They keep Easter with great
enthusiasm, but at the wrong time.  If you belong to
this Church, you had better not visit Russia while the
present government is in power, as Bolshevists regard
the Orthodox Church with a good deal of distaste, and
it is not at all pleasant to be disliked by Bolshevists at
close quarters.

The Anglican Church is more inclusive, and to some
minds more pleasing.  Many people complain that it
lacks authority and apostolic succession, but Anglicans
believe not.  If you are an Anglican, you may be Anglo-
Catholic, Broad, Low, or merely Anglican.  If you
are Anglo-Catholic, you have a congress in the sum-

mer in the Albert Hall, and do not very much care for
English bishops or the Book of Common Prayer. You
read the *Church Times,* and hope for the re-union of
Christendom. (But by Christendom you mean only
the Roman, Orthodox, and Anglican Churches.) You
do not like dissenters, and you regard the office of sung
Matins as a nameless orgy. If you are Broad Church,
you may belong to the Anglican Fellowship or the
Churchmen's Union, contribute to volumes of essays
on religious subjects by different authors edited by
Canon Streeter, read the *Hibbert Journal,* the *Modern
Churchman,* and, if you are very fortunate, become a
Dean. You do not care about Anglo-Catholics, who,
for their part, say masses of reparation for your in-
discretions and existence. You prefer re-union with
the Orthodox Church to re-union with Rome. You
like Higher Criticism. If you are Low Church, you
wish for re-union with Protestant Dissenters, and are
the only people in the world who believe the Thirty-
Nine Articles. You read the *British Weekly* and the
*Record.* If you are just Anglican, you like Sunday
Matins at eleven and services in cathedrals, and do
not wish either for re-union with anyone or for dis-
establishment. You are Church of England.

Then there is Presbyterianism. This religion has
the advantage (if it be one) over the other Protestant
Churches of Great Britain that, north of the Tweed,
its members are not dissenters. Episcopalians are the
dissenters in Scotland. Presbyterians have another advantage: they do not kneel in church, but sit. How-

ever, on the whole they do not have a very good time, for it is thought right that they should attend service on Sundays, and their services are rather long; also, they are supposed to keep the rest of the day rather as the Orthodox Jews keep Saturday, and Sunday games are not played with that openness practised by Anglicans. On the whole, it is a pity to be a Presbyterian unless you are born so. Calvinists are even more unfortunate, as they believe in severe, prolonged, and inevitable punishment after death for nearly everyone, dependent not on conduct in life, but on divine prejudice. If you are unlucky enough to be a Calvinist, you should try hard to believe that you are one of the few exceptions to this rule, and are prejudiced to salvation. Many Calvinists succeed in believing this.

It is much better to be a Quaker. It is very nice to be a Quaker. Quakers say no creeds, so they can believe anything they like. They depend on the light of conscience. They have meetings, at which, if the spirit moves you, you can speak, and say what you like. For the rest of the time you can sit still and think, except when listening to the sayings of your fellow-members. The drawback to being a Quaker is that you have to be very busy with causes and good works; you start funds for the distressed and food centres for the hungry (particularly in Central Europe and specially for those with whom your country has recently had differences), and try to get laws altered. When your country goes to war, as countries from time to time will, you are in an awkward position, and very unpopular, as you think it wrong to fight. Quakers make the best chocolate.

It is more comfortable, in war-time, to be a Christian Scientist, for Christian Scientists do not believe in war. They think that evil, wickedness, and suffering are fancies of ours, and that God does not know anything about them. God did not know about the Great War. Probably He does not know about the Great Peace, either. In fact, such human activities as do come within the sphere of divine knowledge must be very few indeed. It is almost certain that God knows nothing about politics (home or foreign), commerce, laws, house-agents, family life, or, in fact, about the major part of normal human existence. Christian Scientists save money when they are ill by not having doctors. They think highly instead, which is cheaper, and, I dare say, comes to much the same thing in the end.

As to Baptists, Congregationalists, and Wesleyans, the chief thing the ordinary person knows about them is that their places of worship are always (together with the police-station) the ugliest buildings in the village. They often have 1860, 1870, or 1882 engraved upon their walls. They are the kind of architecture that people used to build in those years. They are called chapels, and, if you pass them on a Sunday evening, you will always hear hymn-singing. They have ministers, and at elections they vote Liberal. I do not know why this is. The better-off classes in the country think it ill-bred to be this kind of Dissenter. It

is worst bred of all, I believe, to be a Plymouth Brother.
It is also very sad, as these do not keep Christmas by
so much as a mince-pie.   I once met a Plymouth
Brother, who told me this.   I have never heard what
the advantages of being a Plymouth Brother are.
There must be some, or there would be no Plymouth
Brethren, but all one hears of are its miseries, which
are very great, and which you may find narrated in a
recent novel called *Mary Lee,* a story about a little
Plymouth sister.

Space does not serve me to refer to all the minor
Christian bodies here.   How shall I tell of the Seventh
Day Adventists, the Christadelphians, the Irvingites,
the Swedenborgians, the Mennonites, or the Methusalites?   Of these last two I know only that Mennonites believe in wearing no buttons, and Methusalites
in living as long as they can.   (It was one of the
pathetic ironies of the recent war that several of those
involved in it, and condemned thereby to the polishing
of many buttons and exposure to premature death,
professed membership of one or other of these two
sects.)   The fact is that you can be almost any kind of
Christian.   You can (if you live in Tennessee) even be
a Fundamentalist, or a Holy Roller.

Or you can be a Unitarian.   Often quite cultured
people are Unitarians.   It is a religion suitable for religious persons who cannot believe very much.   If
you are a Unitarian child at a school where the other
children are Church of England, you blush when the

Trinity is mentioned, because you know that your parents are so peculiar as not to believe in it.

If you believe even less than Unitarians do, and yet are still a religious person, you will do well to join the Ethical Church. This sect has a chapel in South Place, Finsbury, and there it meets and worships good behaviour, singing thoughtful hymns about it, and having very civilised addresses, often from eminent persons.

I believe, however, that Positivists believe the least of any of those who meet for worship. But even they believe in acting nobly and living for others, and maxims about this are, or were, inscribed round the walls of their church. Positivists are very religious people, and, though they believe so little, they say quite a lot about it.

The most religious people in the world, however, are Jews. Many Jews by race are free-thinkers, but when a Jew is religious he does it thoroughly. One can see from the Bible how religious Jews are (or were) apt to be. They supplied the world with Christianity, but few Jews are Christians. It is unwise to join the Jewish Church, for Jews have to keep Saturday as a day of rest so rigid that they may not even play a game on it. They have, instead, very long Saturday services. On Sundays they work, so they get no really cheery holiday in the week. You may think (and you will be right) that Jews are very clever and make a lot of money, but do not think that by becoming a Jew you will become clever, for it is not their religion but their race which does it. On the whole, and in spite of being financially fortunate and intelligent, Jews have had a poor time for a good many centuries. They used to be kept in ghettos, and to have their teeth extracted by bad dentists until they gave up their money to the government, and even now they are disliked by many people, such as Mr. Hilaire Belloc. Jews may not eat bacon.

I do not know, either, that you will gain much by being a Buddhist, a Confucian, or a Mahometan, though these religions all have their advantages. Some people are Theosophists, and have many successive lives; others are Mormons and have many simultaneous wives; others are Pagans suckled in a creed outworn, and have many curious gods; others are Pantheists, and worship in the Temple of Nature. It all depends what you want. The choice is wide, and the only really dull thing is to have no religion at all. If you really cannot manage any, you had better instead keep pet dogs, children, or a motor-car. But your life will, whatever you keep, be a shallow affair, lacking background. It is better to have a religion.

# ON THINKING WELL OF OURSELVES

HOW delightful it is to think well of ourselves! Delightful, and surely rather touching, that, after all these æons of not wholly admirable behaviour on the part of the human race, we should still succeed in doing so. That we do so is obvious from the phraseology in which we word our comments on human misconduct. Behaviour of such cunning cruelty that only a human being could have thought of or contrived it we call "inhuman," revealing thus some pathetic ideal standard for our species that survives all betrayals. We admire humanity. "You cur!" we say to those who reveal mean qualities (at least that is what they say in fiction, unless it is "You dog!" "You puppy!" or "You hound!"). Or, "Cat!" we ejaculate; or "Reptile!" or "Swine!"—indicating thus our opinion of the other animals as compared with ourselves. Probably all the animals, in their own manner, do the same. One can fancy the angry dog barking "Man!" at his canine foe; the cat spitting "Woman!" as the final insult to his rival on the slates; the pigs, squealing over their trough, accusing one another of a gluttony so disgusting as only to be called "human." We have no reason to think that we have a monopoly of conceit.

But our conceit does more than embrace the human race. The nations and the sexes proudly claim for

themselves a standard, a quality of nobility, that does
them credit to have conceived. "Manly" is a term of
praise; so is "womanly." "Unmanly," "unwomanly,"
are derogatory adjectives. To be like a man; to be
like a woman; this is very naturally considered by
men and women to imply a high degree of virtue.
As to pride of nationality, it has always been conspicuously in evidence. Recently, the adjective "un-
English" was much to the fore, in discussing the conduct of Continental persons at games. It is un-English
to be unfair at games, or, indeed, at anything else; it is
un-English to bite your foe; to be cowardly, or cruel,
or to lay a hand on a woman save in the way of kindness. In fact, all the meaner vices are called by Eng-
lishmen un-English.

One gathers that they talk in the same way in the
other countries of the world. *"Ce n'est pas fran-
çais,"* is the French comment on cowardice, cruelty,
or treachery. *"Non è italiano,"* say the Italians;
*"Nicht Deutsch,"* the Germans, and the Spaniards *"No
es español." "Facere fortia Romanum est"* the
Romans liked to say (and I daresay do still). The
Hebrew Scriptures are full of expressions of belief
by the children of Israel that, somehow, they were
on a higher plane than their neighbours; and probably they think so still, even as Gentiles do; while from
Russia's snowy plains come wild, conceited cries of
"Un-Cossack! un-Russian! un-Bolshevik! unworthy of
a Ukrainian!" Even in Greenland's icy mountains,
Laps, wrapped in blubber, talk together of the sadly
un-Lap conduct of the less worthy of their community;

and Chinamen condemn one another with "He vellee mean man; he not at all Chink."

More curious than this racial pride is the fact that even the devotees of a game have, in at least one instance, succeeded in imposing on their countrymen the notion that to play this game implies some peculiar virtue. Cricketers have, in their limitless conceit, coined the phrase "Not cricket," and applied it to mean any unfair conduct; and it has been accepted by a meek world, so that you find half the heroes of second-rate novels saying, with unction, "I can't do that; it wouldn't be cricket." I do not know how cricketers have managed this. Footballers, golf-players, hockey, and tennis players, even bridge-players, have failed to impose similar phrases about their favourite pastime. Cricket is no nobler a game than these; its rules are no sterner or more exacting; its code of fair play no higher. Yet, alone among games, cricket has taken its place among the virtues, and not to be cricket has become the eighth deadly sin. And since, to the precisian in language, nothing is cricket except playing a game with a bat, ball, and wickets, this sadly extends the area of sin.

What cricket has done among the games, statesmen have (still more oddly) done among the professions. Among all the strangely used words of the language, "statesmanlike" is, perhaps, the most strangely used. For it is used, as a rule, to mean wise, intelligent, careful, and far-seeing. Personally, I only use it to describe the very worst and most fatuous excesses of diplomacy; but I observe that my use of it is rare.

Most people, even with all the generations of foolish statesmen of history in their minds, even with all the nations noisy with foolish statesmen before their eyes at the present moment, unable as they are even to discover or to call to mind one wise statesman, one single statesman whose statesmanship has done or is doing more good than harm—most people, either in kindness or in blindness, persist in using "statesmanlike" as an adjective of praise. How have statesmen done it? For it must be they who have done it. How, alone among professional men, have these otherwise incompetent persons exalted themselves to this position? What hypnotism have they applied? Members of the other professions—doctors, clergy, writers, lawyers, journalists, actors, bricklayers, nurses, and so forth—have so far failed thus to impose themselves on the world; and yet none of these—no, not even doctors—are so foolish as most statesmen. It must be that statesmen have an even greater supply than most people of self-esteem.

Well, it is all rather pathetic, this tendency of human beings to pose themselves on pedestals in the teeth of all facts. It shows, perhaps, a genuine admiration for the good qualities we claim. It has its touching side; and, however irritating it may be, we must admit that it is, anyhow, human, manly, womanly, English (and characteristic of every other nation, too), statesmanlike, and—in brief—cricket. So it must, I suppose, be all right.

# WHAT THE PUBLIC WANTS

THIS is a topic upon which we, the public, talk a great deal, and rightly. What we want. The desires of humanity and the reasons thereof. What can be more important, more vitally interesting to us all? The question seems to cover a rather wide field of philosophical and metaphysical inquiry, certainly, but that should be no hindrance to any self-respecting journalist such as myself from settling it in a few brief pages.

The public is, of course, all of us. No one, however private he may feel, can evade that common doom of publichood. We are each a head of that monstrous hydra. Well then, what *do* we want? And why? Can we reduce our many million minds, with their many million longings, to any sort of a common appetite? I suppose so. With all our differences, we all want, as the Romans of old did, bread and circuses, and a little drink; we want leisure and comfort, peace and plenty (which means, I suppose, a lot to eat), a little adventure, good company, something to amuse and interest us, money to turn in our pockets; we want to scrape through life with as little annoyance as may be, and to have a rapid and easy death. We want something on which to exercise our faculty of admiration; we want, that is to say, some variant of that which we call beauty. We want success, love, and the appreciation of our fellows; and some of us want to reproduce our kind.

But when it comes to translating these desires into concrete terms, we have not, most of us, much idea of how to do it. We don't know, in fact, what we want; in fact, the majority of us want, or are willing to take, very nearly everything that is offered us. We can be induced to believe that we want almost anything, from war to that Kruschen feeling. In consequence, we are, as Burke put it, the theatre for mountebanks and impostors. We are not particular. We are, in a sense, always that eager, silly, gaping public of the streets, agog for we know not what, ready to run anywhere to see anything—a procession, or a bus accident, or a dead horse. I made part of such a public the other day. Seeing a vast concourse of persons assembled at Oxford Circus, lining the pavements in patient immobility several deep and at least a hundred yards long, all apparently waiting expectantly for something to occur, or pass, or function in some intriguing manner, I inquired of a policeman, as I joined them (not wishing, naturally, to miss anything), what they were hoping to see. His usual expression of benignant contempt increased. "They don't know," he said. "Do none of them know?" I asked. "I shouldn't think so," he replied. "They just stop because they see other people stopping. They don't know what they're doing, or why, half the time." Obviously the public, as viewed by policemen, doesn't know what it wants.

Except that it wants, of course, if it can, to do wrong, to transgress the law in some way. In this it resembles the public as seen by all officials, the public against whom rules are made, who are forbidden to pick the flowers and shrubs, or trespass in woods, or enter the sanctums of station-masters, or take home the books in the British Museum reading-room, or spit in trains. It is obvious what *they* want. They want to do wrong. If officials did not know that we want to do wrong, all these prohibitions would not be put up against us. Viewed by the official mind, we are all miserable sinners, with no health in us. On the other hand, and in spite of this, some kindness is shown us. Sometimes a notice is to be seen announcing that, for the convenience of the public, such and such an arrangement has been made. Sinners we are, but not beyond the pale of treatment by kindness.

Then (I am considering different aspects of the public, the whole being too heterogeneous and giddy a crowd to think about all at once) there is the public as seen by our politicians. To the politician we are something of a dark horse. He does not know what we want; he wishes he did. Do we know ourselves? Vaguely we know that we don't want the politician, that we do want cheap things, no taxes, peace abroad and at home, plenty, a government which interferes with us as little as possible, and no fuss. These large, vague things we want. But do we know which political party will bring us most of them? We do not. We only know that none will bring us much of any of them. We believe, most of us, that one political party is just about as foolish as another, and we rather like to have a House of Commons consisting of three minorities, so that none of them can do anything at all, since we have a well-founded belief that doing is a deadly thing, doing ends in death. We certainly do not want an active government; but what our other political desires are I doubt if most of us know.

And what about that strange, hungry, rapacious creature, the public as seen, or imagined, by the newspaper and magazine editor? There is something a little sinister about this being. Some editors, apparently, see it as a kind of village imbecile, and throw it the provender they believe to be suitable to it. Others believe that there is a public more sophisticated, which wants news of art, politics, literature, and the world at large. But anyone who has ever been asked to write for the cheaper press will have had experiences very significant in the light they cast on what a certain kind of editor believes the public to want. Some time ago, for instance, the literary editor of a newspaper wrote to me asking if I would write an article for his paper on "Why I Would Not Marry a Curate." I rang him up and gave a suitable reply. He said, Well then, would I write about a caveman. I intimated that I was very ignorant of anthropology, and suggested that they should obtain the services of some ethnologist. I was informed that I had mistaken the editor's meaning; what he meant was, not an article on such of our rude forbears as used to live in caves, but on the heroes of the novels of Miss Ethel M. Dell and some of our other contemporary novelists. I said that, unfortunately, I had no acquaintance with the novels to which he referred, so that I could hardly write adequately about the characters contained in them. He said, Well then, would I send him a list of some subjects upon which I could and would write. As the remuneration promised well, I did this. I sent what seemed to me quite a reasonable list of suggestions. But I received a reply saying that I had mistaken his object and the desire of his public, which was to have articles dealing with the lighter side of life. I perceived that by the lighter side of life he meant cavemen, wives, husbands, and marrying curates. Something human, in fact. I felt unable to cope with this, so negotiations were broken off. Shortly afterwards another editor inquired if I would write on "Should Clever Women Marry?" Again I felt unable for the task. Well, there you are. These editors are sure that their public want this kind of stuff. Personally, I believe the editors are quite wrong. I do not believe there is any public which wants anything of the kind. But there is a public which swallows, apparently, anything it gets, and never says what it does want, because it doesn't know. So editors have no resource but to pander to their own morbid taste, hoping that it may also be the taste of others. Those editors who are themselves interested in cavemen, the marriage of clever women, or of members of the Royal Family, or divorces, or

murders, or street accidents, or the week-end occupations of Prime Ministers, or photographs of Prime
Ministers' daughters, or peers' romances, or other
such stuff of life, fill their papers with these things, in
touching and apparently never contravened faith.
Those editors who are more interested in politics, or
strikes, or ancient tombs, or dwindling francs, or the
relations of countries one with another, or the utterances of our legislators in conclave, also attribute these
interests to their readers.   And we, the public, never
say.  We buy, between us, all the papers, all the maga-
zines, we lick it all up, because it's there.  Do we rise
up and say, we want more news of the domestic habits
of the Chinese, or of the stars, or less about cat imprisoned in burning house?  We do not.  Apathetically
we ask for nothing and accept all.  We do not cry
out even against leading articles.  It doesn't follow
that we *read* all that is put before us.  But—and this
is a very solemn thought—there is probably no part of
a paper which someone does not peruse.  Except, possibly, "Why I Would Not Marry a Curate."  I never
heard of anyone outside a newspaper office reading
that.  I do not think any women do.  Women (I
mean by women, of course, women that *are* women,
not—well, not the other kind) read "Why I Should
Not Wash Clothes with Soda," or "Why I Should Not
Give Baby Bacon," or "How to Give My Hair that
Lovely Sheen," or the weather reports—but I think
"Why I Would Not Marry a Curate" panders solely
to the depraved taste of the editor who gets it written.

All the same, no one remonstrates, for we don't know what we want. Stay; now I think of it there is one exception to this rule—we do want and demand "All the Winners."

Let us turn to that public which the producers of slightly less ephemeral literature cater for. That eager, clamorous crowd, for instance, of the novelist's fancy, besieging circulating libraries for his book, or that stupid, perverse herd which haunts his sadder moments, turning their backs on his books, too foolish to know good work when they see it. The novel-reader—that young person cartooned by Mr. Will Dyson, with a book held close to her vacant, silly face, and the eager eyes of the world's novelists concentrated upon her in hope, resolution, delight, fear, or hate. What does she want? That public which, apparently, hails novels by Mr. Joseph Conrad and Miss Ethel M. Dell with almost equal enthusiasm, and yet seems to turn so apathetically away from books of equal worth—what are we to make of it? What does it want? The answer is simple. The majority of the novel-reading public don't know what they want, but can be made to believe that they want almost anything, if told that they ought to do so loudly and often enough by either critics or publishers. All we want is a nice book; you may hear us ask for it at any library. Who are we to know what a nice book is? We can but believe what we are told. If we see *If Winter Comes* written in the sky by an aeroplane, we naturally think *If Winter Comes* must be a nice book. Just as, if we see

Yadil written in the sky by an aeroplane, we naturally think Yadil must be a nice remedy against cancer. Publishers know that, if they say loudly enough and often enough that a book is successful, it soon becomes so. The selling of books is done by publishers, not by the public taste. I believe that publishers could sell in thousands every one of the volumes of nondescript tosh that pour out from their houses if they really gave their minds to it. The public attitude towards novels is very reasonable. We know that scarcely any novels are good—like governments—and that therefore it matters very little which we read. But still, we like to read something, like a nice story to take to bed with us, unless we belong to that lazy, unconventional, sensual, and ill-regulated class of sluggards who do not read in bed, but go straight to sleep—and even these, not caring to confess their sloth, take a book up with them for show. Of course there are novels at which some of us draw the line —our own particular line; but I believe that many readers have no line, but can be induced to read anything. It is only the few who are proud, and say they will read nothing but detective stories, or Jane Austen, or Fielding, or Norman Douglas, or some honest French novel, or whatever their special tipple may be. And even these are liable to fall from their standard and make exceptions. And the majority of fiction readers accept, naturally, whatever comes their way. Vaguely we want a nice book, a witty book, an exciting book, a poetic, imaginative book, a melodrama, but we don't know where to find it, and we take what we can get. If we belong to a circulating library, we ask the attendant young ladies what we should read. "Is this good?" we say. "Shall I like it? Is it light or deep?" "Yes, that's ever so good," reply the obliging girls. "A little on the deep side, but you'll like it." I have never heard them reply, as they must be tempted often to do, "It is not at all good, and therefore I should think, to look at you, you would like it very much. As to the light or deep, it is neither, being like most books, heavy and shallow." No; these kind presiding goddesses always courteously couple together the book's merit and the appreciation of the reader, and send customers away happy with a nice book.

The same with the public that goes to plays. We want a nice play, but we do not know what kind of play is nice. So you get all varieties of plays, of all levels of merit or the reverse, running for long runs or short, and all received by audiences with enthusiasm. "The play was well received": that is the one point on which dramatic critics seem usually agreed, and it is often one of the few true statements they make. We do receive plays well. We like to be at the play. I like it myself. Always I receive plays well. The dramatic critics like it, too, but they do not always say so. You never know what dramatic critics will say. They, like the rest of us, shed their approvals, their disapprovals, on good and bad, with a very beautiful impartiality. The same audience, and the same critics, will praise the wit of Congreve, and that heavy piece of German sentimentality, Faust, and of heavy British sentimentality, what's-its-name. They will blame some bad plays, but let others, no better, pass. They are, like all of us, whimsical creatures, and they have far too many late nights to keep their judgments balanced and cool. Let us not blame them, for neither are we, who have paid for our seats, balanced or cool ourselves. Myself, I am neither, but merely foolishly happy to be at the play, and this is no state of mind for sound criticism. None of us know what we want from the theatre. The critics should not blame the public for not knowing, nor the public the critics for not saying. In this matter of blame, the critics are the worst offenders. Too often they despise the public. "The public," they say, "hates wit and irony." This is a fiction dear to those who believe themselves to be not public but private, and I can only recommend such to listen to any altercation between bus drivers in a London street. The public are indiscriminate, and like nearly everything, and among other things wit and irony. We also like vulgarity and tedious sentimentality. We are most beautifully omnivorous. And no wonder, since the hydra has millions of mouths and each mouth is hungry for different food.

Is there, then, no body of opinion, however small, which knows what it wants and does not want (artistically) and why? Well, I suppose, at any given moment, trained tastes agree, more or less (mostly less), that this is good and that bad. But how fickle is this academy of taste! What it admires changes from decade to decade, almost from day to day. The external wheel spins round. Our fathers despised the wax fruit and horsehair and antimacassars and sham Gothic of our grandfathers. To-day we are beginning again to think these things good. Our Edwardian forbears admired the futurists and cubists. To-day we think these persons crude, and the Sitwells have lately attempted to recanonise Raphael and even to enthrone Carlo Dolci. We are agreed now that Shakespeare wrote well. But was he thought to write well two hundred years ago? He was not. Even landscape is subject to the ups and downs of taste. In the eighteenth century we admired the ordered grove, the shrubbery with statues, the dædal earth and the pœcile park, and swooned to think of mountains. In the early nineteenth century mountains came in with romance, and fed the Victorians' dark Byronic moods. In our return to-day to the eighteenth century it is possible that the trim landscape may have again its turn, together with Pope, Addison, and the coffee-house wits. No; there is no fixed standard of taste. Æsthetically there may be good, there is certainly bad. As Browning put it, there may be heaven, there must be hell—but has mankind ever been of a mind as to which is which? And we, the great public, not trying to solve that Platonic riddle, fall back agreeably and with an admirable impartiality on liking very nearly everything. And quite right too.

## WOMAN: I. HER TROUBLED PAST

ALAS, poor woman! At last the full tale of her griefs down the ages has been unfolded by a sympathetic pen. Mr. W. L. George has written a brief and compendious history of her, a tragedy of forty thousand years in fifty thousand words. A tabloid tragedy; potted pains for the people. It was a great enterprise, and one is not surprised to note that Mr. George consulted a bibliography ranging from Mr. H. G. Wells to Sir James Frazer, from Boccaccio to the Bible, from Gibbon and Dr. William Smith to Mr. Lytton Strachey and "The Heir of Redclyffe." He gives us a good deal of brightly condensed information, all of it pointing to the same conclusion, that woman has been most unfortunate, not merely twice, like the countess in *The Grand Duchess,* but every time and all the way. "The picture," says Mr. George, in effect, every few pages, "is one of unrelieved horror." "Thus," he comments, "continues the long tale of woman's misery." One feels by the end of the book (though a gleam of hope is offered us here, for Mr. George believes in Progress, Hope, and the Future) that this unhappy creature, who has trodden so bitter a road for so many centuries with such a delusive air of gaiety, has not had her meed of pity.

Speaking as a woman, I may say that I feel defrauded. I had not known that my plight was so sad; I had not guessed at the misery of my mother, my grandmothers, my great-grandmothers, all my distressed ancestresses back to the she-ape. Those of them I have known have seemed, on the whole, so cheerful. . . . Of course one knows that this is a vale of tears, and that man (and woman) is born to trouble as the sparks fly upward, but this dictum applies to both sexes, whereas it is women who, Mr. George points out, have down the ages suffered more grief than they could tell, and men who have inflicted it.

A great deal of Mr. George's indictment of society is quite just and accurate. Laws, he says, have from the earliest times until quite lately been unjust to women. Of course. Laws are always unjust to everyone, both in the earliest times and the latest. That is what laws are for. Some of them have, certainly, been more unjust to women than to men—the divorce laws, for instance. But Mr. George is not fair in effect, though accurate, when he complains that, in the early part of last century, poor women could be hanged, publicly whipped, or stood in the pillory. They could; but so could poor men. Mr. George would perhaps reply that he never said they couldn't, but that he happened just now to be writing a history of women. All the same, as he puts it, it sounds as if this savagery had been a special trouble of women, whereas it was not a sex trouble at all, but a human one, and incidentally a class one.

Human beings have always treated one another with abominable savagery, both within and without the law, but have women been more savagely treated than men? Edward III, says Mr. George, imprisoned his mother for twenty-eight years. But would not he, or any other monarch, have imprisoned his father with even greater joy had he acceded to power while his father yet lived? Imprisoning one's mother is not really an anti-feminist act, though it is both barbarous and impertinent. Again, Mr. George complains that a Hebrew father sacrificed his daughter as a burnt offering. But what about Abraham, who required the intervention of an angel from heaven to keep him from similarly disposing of Isaac? A Levite once cut a woman in twelve pieces. But surely the pieces into which male Hebrews were cut must, in sum total, be in number as the sands of the sea. There was no anti-feminism here. Mr. George should be fair. But he gives other indications of having misunderstood those passionate woman-lovers, the Palestine Jews; he says, for instance, that "A woman was chosen as wife not so much for her beauty as because of her qualities —humility, frugality, or charity." He should read the Song of Solomon, which does not exclaim, "Behold, thou art frugal, my beloved, behold, thou art humble."

The Bible is full of such personal admirations; of how Mr. Dash saw Miss Blank, that she was fair, and desired her, and either took her forthwith or made patient suit to her. Mr. George is inclined to misjudge human nature in this matter; he says, for instance, that "to the early Greeks, a woman was a woman, as a chair is a chair." But how improbable! And how at variance with the evidence of literature on this subject! The early Greeks were not such fools. However women may have been treated, one may be sure that the ability to discriminate between one and another of them has always been found among men. One may be sure also that, if this indiscriminateness of taste ever existed, it cut both ways, and that to the women of the same period a man was a man. Let us give men here, too, their fair grievance.

We pass to the Middle Ages. "The position of woman was tragic in the early Middle Ages, a period filled with strife." But surely strife is even more tragic for men. It would be truer to say that everyone's position was tragic in that dark period, and especially the position of the poor. But such ladies as the Wife of Bath seem to have been cheery enough, anyhow, and not unduly weighed down by tragedy. As to the lack of learning which Mr. George ascribes to women throughout the sixteenth and seventeenth centuries, he should look up the education of Lady Jane Grey, Margaret Roper (*née* More), and other young females. It might suggest to him one feminine trouble that he has omitted.

Mr. George tends throughout to under-estimate the amount of education received by women. He writes thus of the mid-Victorian wife: "To read her Bible, tend her children, sing to her man" (here is a heavy trouble for men, by the way), "this seemed to make up her simple philosophy. . . . Almost invariably uneducated, sometimes practical, but never much of a friend." Shades of our grandmothers! Has (one wonders) Mr. George consulted his before writing this passage? Of my own great-grandmothers, one, at least, was at home in Greek, Latin, and Hebrew, as well as the modern European languages, another grounded all her sons in the classics to prepare them for their public schools. And those grandmothers of ours, those lively, brilliant, sharp-tongued ladies—did they indeed "recognise their sphere as being to cook, to look after children, and to please men"? One may imagine their retorts if one had asked them. . . .

Mr. George seems like many people to have some inaccurate ideas of the last century. He speaks of the "Victorian blight," calls the Victorian age reactionary, and says that the great men of the time despised their period. Well, have not all great men despised all periods, which are, in point of fact, for the most part despicable? And was the Victorian period, so alive with invention, intellectual activity, speculation, scientific thought and discovery, poetry, literature, and philosophy, really so despicable as most others? But Mr. George, rather arbitrarily, says that he will call what was good in this period "nineteenth century." "And so," he says, "let us say Victorian Age when we mean everything that is hypocritical, dull, and meanly sensual." Well, of course, one can say anything. Let us say, "the age of George the Fifth" when we mean everything that is silly, sentimental, and stupid, and "twentieth century" when we refer to the period's brighter aspects. What's in a name?

Nor, surely, can Mr. George be right in saying that "social life from 1880 to 1890 was a heavy affair." He should read Lady Oxford's autobiography; he should consult his parents as to the London of those days. One has always been given to understand that never was such a brilliant galaxy of men and women entertaining one another. "Woman," says Mr. George, "was growing educated; she rebelled against conjugal authority, and took to cigarettes or 'The Yellow Book' as a protest." But why "The Yellow Book" (which by the way, did not appear until 1894)? In what sense could the perusal of that prettily-got-up, prettily-written, but rather feeble, dull, and young-ladyish periodical be regarded as a protest against anything? As to cigarettes, our mothers probably smoked them for the same reason that we do—because they liked them. And how, again, can smoking be a protest, unless you smoke in a non-smoking compartment, a church, or a lift? Taking to smoking was no more, one imagines, a protest when women did it in 1890 than when men did it in 1620.

But what Mr. George means is that women at this time were coming on. Dark was their lot, but less dark than before. There was more hope for the world. "Religion was being questioned, while ethics were not yet adopted." (As a matter of fact, religion had been questioned for a few thousand years, and ethics had been adopted in theory—they have never been so in practice—by our first ancestors who could think.) Finally, "it was a period of magnificent intellectual activity, when it was possible at last to pronounce the words 'free love' and 'socialism' without being excluded from human society." For this disarming picture of intellectual activity, I could forgive Mr. George more disagreements with myself than I find in this book.

He ends on a note of hope. Women will shake off all trammels and advance. He does not say whether men will do so too. Human beings are an unfortunate race, hindered and hampered on every side. Let us spare pity for both sexes, and not spend it all on women, for, after all, in most respects, men and women have always been in the same boat, suffering from *mal de mer* together on the waves of this troublesome world.

# WOMAN: II. HER DARK FUTURE

IT is not altogether easy to think seriously upon this great subject. Few topics, indeed, are easy to think seriously about, and the future of men and women (I find it difficult to separate the probable destinies of the two creatures) is certainly not among these. For, consider, it is only too probable that women (and men) have no future at all, are going nowhither, are, in brief, merely going out, like little candles lighted for a moment in chaos. They may not see the sun rise after this night in which I write.

On the other hand, they may. It is a sporting event, this continued life of living creatures upon this so precarious planet. They may be all knocked out next round by the blind forces of a turbulent universe, and seen no more. Perhaps it would be for the best?

But personally I lay odds on women and men having some kind of a future after to-day, if only a short one. As I say, I do not find it easy to consider the future of women apart from that of men. I find it no easier than to speculate on the future of mares, apart from the destiny of horses. Doubtless, whatever strange doom is in store for each species will be shared by both sexes.

What kind of future then, if any, awaits woman? We have many data to work upon. We have, in brief, her past. We look back to the dim dawn of human life upon this planet, and see the female of the species swinging blithely from tree to tree with the infants of the species clasped in her hairy arms. We see her a little later, chattering, voluble, affectionate, absurd, cuffing and feeding the children, decorating the home and her person with gaudy flowers, while her mate seeks ravening after his prey. She cooks the prey, clothes the children in skins, offers sacrifices to the fearful gods, chatters and gossips about the village, pursues the avocations and the amusements of the hour, throwing up a continuous smoke-screen, then as now, between the vivid moment and the dark annihilation that awaits all human activities.

A cheerful creature, on the whole, with sound tastes; tastes, that is, for food, drink, talk, companionship, gay colours, music, love, and jokes. A creature (in both its male and female aspects) very like a monkey still, as, indeed, it is to-day. More and more it decks itself in beautiful garments, hanging bright jewels from its person, combing its hair, pleasing itself and its mate by what is, according to the very peculiar standards of the race (for if each species did not admire itself physically, where would love and the family be?), considered beauty. And all the time queer, disturbing new forces were and are assaulting the creature's soul.

Those who keep themselves informed on social topics declare that these forces have of late—that is to say, during the past seventy years or so—brought about a great change in the position of human females upon this globe. They are doubtless correctly informed. It certainly seems true that various professions which formerly, for some reason or reasons, did not admit women, now do so. It also seems true that there is less check on the doings of women: no longer are they frowned upon for practising the simple human activities. (One has forgotten now why this ever occurred—probably there was no reason.) They enjoy more of what is called *liberty*. But all human creatures enjoy so very little of this that such advance seems hardly noticeable to the philosophic eye. Still are we, both men and women, hemmed about on every side, prevented in nearly all our doings, by the paternal governments which rule over us and by the exigencies of convention.

We still remain savages, with the savage's laws and taboos. But it is true that we are less savage than we were, and that the physically weaker sex has profited by the modification of barbarism. Will it continue to profit? Indeed, will barbarism continue to modify, or will it gain some monstrous victory and send the human race hurtling back to scratch?

If it should continue to modify, how will women be affected? Will they become ever more intelligent and professional, ever less parasitic, work hard and ever harder (horrid doom!) in the interests of their own maintenance and that of their young? Will married women be expected, even as married men, to contribute towards the upkeep of the family? Will an idle, kept woman become as much an object of contumely as an idle, kept man? Will there be enough jobs to go round? Will the voice of woman in the laws and counsels of the nations make these laws and counsels yet more unintelligent and depraved than they now are?

Myself, I can answer none of these questions but the last. It will not. For nothing could lower the intellectual level of the laws and counsels of the nations. Far be it from me to suggest that the assistance of women will raise it, but at least it cannot reduce it. There is comfort in that thought.

As to the rest, it is too difficult. Though I suppose I might write about it, as about anything else, I cannot think about it. I do not know enough. When anyone says to me "Where is woman going?" or "Where is man going?" all my dazzled eyes can see is man and woman sailing mazily and precariously through the kingdoms of the air. A fresh medium of transport: that is all I see. Apart from mechanical devices, futures show, as a rule, a remarkable resemblance to pasts.

It is a pity that we shall never know. We are still primeval men and women, and we cannot peer through the mist which divides us from modern woman and modern man. But I confess that I do not care for them. I cannot like Posterity. With all their accomplishments, they seem to me a little crude. As doubtless we seemed to our still more primeval ancestors. Perhaps the less said about it all the better.

# A PLATONIC AFFECTION

SOME years ago the *Times* invited and received correspondence about the reasons for the vast success of a recent popular novel. I remember that many correspondents suggested as the main reason that the novel in question relates the story of a true Christian, of God's Good Man doing his duty against odds. "Its issues are spiritual," wrote one correspondent. "The hungry sheep are fed." He proceeded to draw a moving picture of a huge public despising the selfishness and trickeries of the world in which they move, and finding in this book "an escape into nobler issues." "Can it be," he inquired (but not incredulously, for he was sure that it could), "that the reading world discerns in this Mark Sabre a real man, or, shall I say, a Christian, who, without preaching, without fuss, lives the Sermon on the Mount against all odds?" Setting aside the application of this view to the popularity of this particular novel (and it would hardly explain it, for we find an equally high degree of virtue in very many novels which yet do not achieve success), it is an interesting question which is here raised. How far is right conduct what a large majority of persons want to hear and read about? And does this account for the popularity of the Christian Gospels? And for

the realisation of politicians that Right against Wrong
is nearly as good a fighting cry as Cheaper Bread, or
Our Country for Ever, and that the best way to fill
recruiting offices is to give out that the war on hand
is between Christ and anti-Christ, honour and knavery,
virtue and vice? And for the tendency of newspapers
to large-type headlines about "Courageous Conduct
of Young Woman," "Self-Sacrifice of Dog," "Mother
Gives Yard of Own Skin to Save Child's Life," and
so forth? And for the nearly inevitable triumph,
on the stage, of virtue over vice? And for the claim
made by many people to the possession of ethical
qualities of one sort or another? "I am naturally
frank and truthful, and of an open, generous temper,"
the autobiographist will write, and it does not strike
us as strange that they seldom say instead, "I am a
liar ingrain, and of a mean and miserly habit." It
does not strike us as strange, because it is merely the
tribute (paid crudely, but in the only way they know)
of the human race to virtue. "Good." It is a curious word, vastly various in meaning, and has been
always much discussed. Good wine, good food, good
music, good art, good literature, good weather, good
conduct. . . . Some of these we enjoy, and not others.
Some noble mentalities enjoy all of them. The least
widely, if the most intensely admired are good music,
art, and literature. These are the reward of the few.
Does conduct rank with food, wine, and weather as
a department of life in which goodness is almost universally admired? Not, of course, attained; like good

food and wine, it is, as a rule, too costly for that—but all the more admired for its very inaccessibility.

It is a strange thought. Strange, indeed, that this odd, flying fragment we call earth, spinning so crazily, so precariously in space, like a child's ball on a string, that may at any moment break loose and fly off at a tangent into illimitable space, to meet at last a horrid end in the fiery maw of some monstrous devouring sun—strange that this irresponsible, unwholesome ellipse, originating who knows how, bound none knows whither, breaking all over its surface into fetid vegetation and horrid, gelatinous life, life running on myriads of legs, on four, on two, on none, should have broken also into this infinitely paradoxical life of the spirit. Man, in the beginning a gluttonous, self-preserving, unethical protoplasm, living plain and thinking plainer, has somehow, in the course of his quest for higher living, found higher thinking, too, and that most strange apprehension that we call a sense of ethics. No amount of investigation into the origins of moral ideas, no amount of discovery that they are, one and all, utilitarian in basis, evolving out of the tribal sense of the welfare of the community, will really explain this thing. Most of the virtues themselves may be explained as utilitarian evolutions, but not the profound admiration we accord them, not the romantic thrill with which we greet feats of heroism, devotion, self-sacrifice, and generosity. In an almost wholly queer world, this phenomenon is one of the queerest. Why do we admire the courageous fling-

ing away of life, the sacrifice of happiness for the sake
of an ideal, the devoted love of one person towards
another, all the heroic, inconvenient, unutilitarian
pagan and Christian virtues? Stranger paradox still
—if we do indeed admire them, why do we not practise
them, so as to have a stage always before our eyes
set with the objects of our admiration? The answer
to that is, no doubt, that this would be too costly a
process: many things which we admire we must do
without. With true unselfishness, we prefer to admire
virtue in others.

And yet, side by side with the paragraphs in the
newspapers about noble deeds, we have "Cocaine
Orgy," "Murder in a Hotel." And the hungry sheep
swallow these stories of wickedness with even more
avidity than that with which they devour tales of
virtue. The sheep like virtue, but they also like the
horrid: it feeds some appetite in them. Perhaps it is
the same appetite which craves also to hear of virtue,
perhaps it is another. "Femme Coupée en Morceaux"
—as the French papers remark in large and cheerful
headlines, rightly, and, knowing their sheep, giving
these grisly happenings prominence over other European
events. Is it merely that the sheep want excitement,
that any kind of a thrilling tale goes, be it of virtue
or of vice? Raffles is a popular figure as well as the
Third Floor Back, Robin Hood the highwayman, as
well as Sir Philip Sidney the gentleman, the murderer
as well as the philanthropist, Mephistopheles as well
as Christ. If we cannot get virtue, vice does: both

begin with a "v"; further, both are within the region
of ethics. A bad man or a good—one or the other
we like, and, if possible, both in the same drama,
pitted one against the other. But it is, in the main,
to the good that our hearts go out.

It may surely be regarded by moralists as a hopeful
symptom, this romantic admiration, however platonic
and sentimental it may be, however lacking in that
desire for union which some hold to be the essence of
love, and however paradoxical a business it makes life
as normally lived appear. A fancy, a barren flirtation,
if you will . . . but still, there, for what it is worth,
it is.

# CRANKS

WHAT are cranks? Wishing to know (for, personally, I never know what any word means), I have been inquiring in various quarters and have received various replies. The Oxford Dictionary says that a crank (in a figurative meaning) is "a person with a mental twist, especially one who is enthusiastically possessed by a particular crochet or hobby; an eccentric, or monomaniac." And an early Victorian gentleman whom it cites calls them, more severely, "persons of disordered mind, in whom the itch of notoriety supplies the lack of higher ambition." These two definitions seem a little incompatible; one who is enthusiastically possessed by a crochet or hobby does not usually suffer from the itch of notoriety; the itch of collecting stamps, eggs, or autographs, or of abolishing meat, war, vivisection, crime, punishment, disease, or hats, is, as a rule, itch enough for one person. Crankiness and ambition are not a good team to drive together. Ambitious persons are out for this world's goods; cranks are out for some strange ideal in their own minds; their kingdom is not of this world.

Nearer the truth than the Victorian gentleman was the person who said, "A crank is the handle which makes the machine go." Go where? That does not really matter, and is perhaps better not inquired into. Anyhow, go somewhere; be a dynamic machine, not a static.

A usual definition during the last war, was "Cranks? Oh, they want peace, don't they?"— They wanted peace, that is, so immoderately that it became what is theologically termed an inordinate affection. Twenty years ago it was, "They want votes." Twenty years hence it may be, "They want war." Indeed, unsatisfied desire appears to be of the essence of crankism. Satisfy desire, give your cranks their peace, their votes, their war, their nuts, and they cease to be cranks. Florence Nightingale was accounted a crank while she only desired to go and nurse the sick. When she had achieved this desire she was called a Noble Woman, a Lady with a Lamp, and other opprobrious names, but no longer a crank. Further, the desire of the crank must be based on theory and reason, not on mere appetite and liking. Which reminds me of another definition. "Cranks? Oh, good gracious, I knew a woman who had a cold.poached egg in the night whenever she woke. *She* was a crank." I inquired if she performed this ritual because she liked cold poached eggs, or for some other reason, and was told that it was because she maintained that wakefulness was caused by lack of albumen in the system. Since that was her reason, I was prepared to admit her into the circle of cranks. If she had taken the poached egg (as I believe H.M. King Edward VII was used to do on similar occasions) merely because she liked it, because it comforted her when in the night she sleepless lay, she would not have been a crank, but a simple human animal. Cranks live by theory, not by pure desire. They want votes, peace, nuts, liberty, and spinning-looms not because they love these things, as a child loves jam, but because they think they ought to have them. That is one element which makes the crank. Another is lack of proportion, the obsession with one desire or one principle to the minimising or exclusion of others; exaggeration, in fact. People are not cranks if the cause they have at heart is so important that its importance cannot be exaggerated. If it is, for instance, education, beauty, morality, religion, housing, or international peace, they may be enthusiasts, but they are not cranks. You may, for instance, be a crank on the subject of wanting a vote, because you may exaggerate the importance of a vote as such. But you cannot be a crank about the things which you believe that a vote represents and will help you to procure; about these things your enthusiasm will make of you a more dangerous thing—a fanatic.

To sum up, the main body of cranks may be divided into two parties—the pioneers, who will be the normal of to-morrow, and the retrogrades, who were probably the normal of the day before yesterday. There is also a section of them which is the normal, we may believe, not of time but of eternity, of these are the saints; and another section which is the normal, one imagines, of Colney Hatch. It takes all sorts of cranks to make this interestingly mixed world.

## UNKNOWN COUNTRIES

HOW do other people live? We do not know. No one knows. Those strange little foreign countries, each barred behind frontiers across which no passport carries aliens—what fantastic adventures, what romantic paths, what sad and gay portents and marvels, are to be found therein? What, in brief, are the hourly, the daily, the yearly lives of our fellow-creatures? As I have remarked (and it cannot be too strongly emphasised), we do not know. None of our manifold and profound human ignorances is more abysmal than this ignorance of the lives led around and on all sides of us. Novels, which ought, being stories about human lives, to help us, do not. For the writers of these stories are, as a rule, ignorant themselves. Do novels tell us of the daily life of the stockbroker, the bank clerk, the actor, the school-mistress, the clergyman, the prime minister, the nurse, the nun? They do not. They do not show us brokers broking, clerks banking, actors acting, teachers teaching, statesmen governing, nurses nursing, cooks cooking, solicitors soliciting, deans deaning, nuns nunning; they only tell of the lives of these persons when off duty, their emotions, thoughts, and such, which are common to us all. They deal, mostly, with what is extraneous to the professions of their characters; they show us the stockbroker in the home, bankrupt and in the act of committing suicide, or flourishing in wicked wealth, and planning non-professional villainies against young ladies; the bank clerk not embezzling, but only having embezzled; the solicitor being called on by hero or heroine—just a little vignette out of his long day flashed on to the page; the statesman not governing but conversing in salons, having (we assume) governed earlier in the day, the dean not deaning but being pompous in his home, the nun not nunning but desiring to cease nunning. We do not see the business man or the civil servant performing business in his office; we see him only after office hours, when he has left the City or Whitehall for his home in Mayfair or the suburbs. So we are none the wiser as to how, in detail, they practise their daily avocations. We never learn what bank clerks do in those mystic hours between 3:30 and 5, after they have ceased to inquire how we will have it, but by no means (we are told) ceased to toil. We are not told (except by Mr. Compton Mackenzie, who has done good service in this matter) of the daily round of the vicar or the curate; we only see these clergymen, for the most part, in their off-hours. It should, I think, be a law (there are many laws even more unjust) that everyone should write and publish, at the public expense, once in their lives a detailed journal of their year, with daily records of their activities. Then we should know.

Not long ago, a young man who had very recently

been an undergraduate spoke to me of the wives and the daughters of University dons. The wives of dons had, he said, but one interest and occupation—the collection of undergraduates for lunch and tea parties. They regarded undergraduates, he said, as scalps. The daughters of dons had, further to this, he said, a second aim in life—to become the wives of dons. Their lives, he said, during vacation time were arid wastes of boredom and misery. General or intellectual interests they had none. As a one-time don's daughter, I informed him that he was in error on this matter, and that the female relatives of dons were quite normal persons, leading ordinary, rational lives, interested in the activities and the society of the place in which they lived, and in those outside it, given to intellectual pursuits, games, the arts, or any other normal, trivial human interests. I did not like to add what is, in fact, the truth, that his so-called "collection of undergraduates" is a tedious social obligation performed by most dons' wives in the bored yet stoical spirit in which the viear's wife gives parish parties. In any case, he did not believe me. The simple child would have his way; he had passed nine terms in the same town with these persons, and he knew them to be many minds with but a single thought, and that thought undergraduates. To him their lives were so many foreign countries into which he had never set foot. They had asked him to tea; so that, to him, was their only aspect; just as some people think that the whole business of the flea is to bite them, not knowing of this little creature's wonderful and intelligent activities in private life and between meals.

This young man may have been more foolish than most of us, in that he invented where he did not know; but was he more ignorant? Read the novels written by the rich about the poor, by the literate about the illiterate. What travesties of human life and speech do they one and all set forth! Read novels about schoolmistresses by those who have not been school-mistresses, or about detectives and criminals by those who have been neither. With what wild fantasies do their pages burgeon! Hear the poor on the lives of the rich. "Trouble," said one poor woman, "isn't so hard to bear for you rich people, because you can always touch the bell and in comes a mutton chop." Her general thesis was, indeed, accurate; trouble *is* easier, infinitely easier, for the rich than for the poor; but her picture of a day spent by the bereaved rich in touching the bell and consuming mutton-chops was a happy and fictitious dream, as wide of the mark as the pictures of the lives of the poor drawn by, say, Thomas Hardy, those of politicians by Mrs. Humphry Ward, of guardsmen by Ouida, of doctors by Sir Arthur Conan Doyle.

What lies behind all those ugly, interesting human masks which surround me in the dawdling omnibus? What strange paths, for ever unknown to me, have their feet this day pursued and will again pursue, when chance, having thus flung us randomly for a moment together, shall fling us once more apart, and we shall go our several ways, strangers yet? I understand no one of those hidden lives, excepting only that of the conductor, whose profession is, indeed, open to the eye. (That of the driver is also so open, but his mind is so far above mine that he must be accounted among the mysteries.)

Where do flies go in the winter time? What do Lamas do when not visiting Europe, bishops when not confirming or ordaining, telephone operators when not apologising for having tr-r-oubled us?

No one knows. We can only exercise our human prerogative of charity, and hope for the best.

# THE TRUTH

# IF WE TOLD IT

W E may well inquire, on hearing the word "truth" mentioned—What is truth? Or rather, which of the many kinds of truth is here referred to? For no word has more (though most have as many) meanings. By truth you may mean the nature of things as they are; or the approximate agreement of human words with what we conceive to be fact; or the natural disposition found in some human beings to attempt to achieve such agreement; or the resemblance of a work of literature or art to the objects or emotions described or portrayed; or the correct working of a machine; or about fifty other things. Keats, oddly, meant beauty—or said in a moment of verse that he did. In their variety of interpretations and applications, the words "truth" and "true" are almost as manifold as the words "honesty" and "honest." An honest man, honest mirth, honest doubt, my honest fellow, to be made an honest woman, honest English cooking—what a medley of meanings is here! The fact is that we have (though they seem a great many) too few words, and so have to stretch each to cover ground not properly belonging thereto.

As to truth, I am meaning by it here (for the purposes of the moment and of this article) not that pearl of great price that lies hid deep, to be dug for toil-

fully and in vain, nor that shadowy form at the bottom
of wells, eluding always our dipping pails; but merely
that purveyance of correct information by one human
being to another which we call Speaking the Truth.
And it may as well be admitted at once that this can
very seldom be done. A thousand difficulties prevent
it. The inadequacy of the human language, the in-
accuracy of the human mind, the havoc wrought in
social life by any such attempt, the ruptures of friendship, the stabs to love, the injury to commerce, the
death to political life—all these make any noticeable
degree of truth-telling either impossible or undesirable,
and often both.

Consider, for instance, the life of an ordinary private
person, and what havoc complete truth would work
in it. Directly we enter into contact with our fellows,
deceit begins. We have perhaps, at breakfast, letters
asking us to do this or that. Either we must consent
(an extreme step to take), or we must politely refuse.
We are invited perhaps to deliver a lecture, or to go
to the house of someone of our acquaintance in order
to eat a meal or gather at some gathering or meeting
or even bazaar. Were we truthful, we should write
back: "Thank you very much; it is kind of you to
ask me to go to your house (or other spot appointed)
for this purpose, but I do not care to, and so will not."
Not being truthful, we say we are so sorry but we
cannot come. This is a lie, since we are not sorry
and we could. But it is a lie that makes no ill feeling,
whereas the truth would certainly give offence. Our

morning post probably contains several such lies sent us
by others. There may well, too, be letters from makers
or sellers of merchandise. What do these say? Not,
"I do not really think that what I want to sell is much
good or at all cheap, and there are many better such
goods on the market; but still, I would like you to buy
mine, as I should gain money over the transaction."
No; they say instead: "Dear Sir, or Madam,—It is
by now universally admitted that my wines, cigars,
motor-cars, insurance policies, remedies for influenza,
or what not, are the best on the market and the most
moderate in price." Sometimes they add, "If the
goods do not give satisfaction, same will be accepted
back and money returned." This is a black lie. The
whole letter is a lie. But it is all put so nicely, so
soothingly, that the odds are that, if ever you should
find yourself in want of that kind of merchandise, you
will send for the brand mentioned in the letter. Anyhow, it is very certain that you would not send for
the goods of a truthful tradesman. You would think
that, if *that* were all he could find to say of his wares,
same must indeed be a poor lot.

So much for lies at breakfast. (But I have not
even mentioned the morning newspaper; it would take
too long.) And so it is throughout the day. Without
attempting to follow the business or professional man
to his duties, conducted, doubtless, with varying degrees of duplicity, consider for a moment the house-
wife. She goes shopping perhaps. What do those
who serve her in shops say to her? "Cod is nice

to-day," says the fishmonger. A lie. Cod is never nice, and well he knows it. And, were cod nice, it would not be nicer one day than another. Why should it? "Nice weather to-day," says the draper, mechanically, not troubling to glance at the chill, murky skies. That is nearly always, in this country, a lie. Lately people have been saying, "Invigorating weather!"— referring to the deathly cold that saps all vigour and all life. "We don't get asked for that shade ever," says the lofty milliner who lacks a colour; "it's not worn this year"—and the shopper turns away mortified, even though she knows it to be a lie. But, "That hat suits madam very well," says another, and confidence returns; for if *that* hat suits madam, madam must have the kind of face that any hat will suit.

We need not follow madam throughout her devious day. Deceiving and deceived, morally and intellectually incapable of accuracy, she and her male fellow-liars, in private life and in public, in the office and in the home, with the tongue, the pen, and the printed word, weave day and night the tortuous mists of error which make the atmosphere of human life upon this planet. It is doubtless for the best. Without these mists the bleak air of truth, of accurate statement of facts and inclinations and emotions as they are, would perhaps strike too raw and sharp upon lungs used to an atmosphere of illusion. We should feel like French travellers when an open train window lets in upon their comfortable snugness a *courant d'air*. It would not do.

# A MAN WHO TOLD IT

"THE people of England," said the chairman, not for the first time that week, "the people of West Midshire, are asking for the truth. And they will vote for that man and that party who gives it them. Here is your candidate, Mr. Robinson, coming before you with a plain, truthful tale, and no trickeries. The truth, the whole truth, and nothing but the truth—that's what Mr. Robinson has to give you, ladies and gentlemen, and if you want something else you must go somewhere else for it. Mr. Robinson will now address you."

For the twenty-first time that week Mr. Robinson found himself on his feet facing a cheering audience. An exquisite sensation—but how short-lived! Would that the gratifying noise could go on for ever. But it always ceased, and then one had to make noises oneself. One had to work oneself up to a vigorous, believing, racy mood, and pour forth one's tale of how right was one's own party, how very wrong the others. Mr. Robinson had done so twenty times that week, and was prepared to do so again to-night. But, as he stood there on the platform of the chilly, ugly parish hall, above the rows of patient, ugly faces (for the human face, at its best, is assuredly ugly, and not less so in West Midshire than elsewhere), a strange seizure de-

scended upon him.   The truth, the chairman had said.
The people of England were asking for the truth.   If
that were indeed so, why not, for once, give it them?
The truth, the whole truth . . . no, not the whole
truth; no one had ever known or told that; it was a
nonsensical phrase . . . and nothing but the truth.
Well, then, they should *have* nothing but the truth.
One would discover whether the chairman was right.

A shining vision of Truth hovered before Mr. Robinson's spectacled eyes like the Holy Grail.   He dis-
carded his well-worn openings, and dropped deep, down
and down into the well of his ignorant and ill-informed
mind, for the sentences which should most accurately
word his real position in this matter of party politics.
The first thing he discovered was that he must retract
a great number of things which he had on other occasions said, and which he did not really believe.

He began slowly, haltingly, throwing his mind in-
ward upon himself, instead of out towards his hearers.

"I am standing," he said dreamily, "as a Liberal.   I
don't quite know why.   I am on the whole in favour of
Free Trade, after such inadequate study of the matter
as my untrained and not very intelligent mind has allowed of.   But I am not an economist.   I think that
Protection would raise prices and hinder trade, but I
don't feel certain.   I do not think that it would help
unemployment much, but again I do not know.   I am
not clever enough to know.   Very few people are.
Neither am I sure that the Labour programme is necessarily worse than the others.   I do not think that any

party is likely to improve to any great extent either un-employment or bad trade. The Liberal methods of attacking these problems do not seem to me to be much better than the Conservative or Labour methods; all are very bad.

"I am afraid that I do not regard my party, or any other party, as either honest or competent. They are mostly rather stupid men; the politician is apt to have a second-rate mind, or rather a mind which becomes second-rate directly it is applied to politics. The fact is that the management of the home and foreign affairs of a country is too difficult a business for anyone to do at all well. No one ever has done it well, and no one ever will. And whichever party gets into power at this election will doubtless do it very badly. But there you are; someone has to get in. I ask you, my friends, to vote Liberal, on no grounds that I can think of except that I should like to be returned. I should like to be in Parliament. It is not true what I have sometimes said at meetings, that I do not want for my own sake to be in Parliament, but feel that I ought. I do not believe that I should be of the least use in Parliament, but I would like to be there. That is, my friends, the one definitely affirmative statement I am able to make to you to-night. It is a foolish and useless profession, that of politics, like most others, but I should enjoy it. All the same, I can think of no reason why you should vote for me, unless you, as I do not, definitely hold that one party programme is better than another. If you do, you are fortunate.

"I fear that I have said, at other meetings, and even in my printed addresses, that I represent the plain man and woman. Let me say now that I have no idea what I meant by this, as I do not know what a plain man or woman is. The reverse, I suppose, of a complicated man or woman. But the complication or otherwise of our mentality does not affect our economic interests and position; so I repeat that I meant nothing at all by the foolish phrase. I said also, I believe, that I relied on the plain voter to go quietly to the polls and vote for me. I confess that I do not see why he should vote more quietly than his opponents who vote for Mr. Wilkins and Mr. Jones. I have said a number of very foolish things in the past, but I now unsay them all. To-night I will give you nothing but the truth as I see it.

"Now first about this question of Free Trade and prosperity, a question about which I am really very ignorant . . ."

Mr. Robinson, rapt in a new and strange freedom, isolated, as it were, on a little lonely island, from which he spoke stumblingly through mists, unconscious of the world around him, was recalled to ordinary life by a note thrust into his hand. Looking round, he saw the agitated face of his agent. He read the note. "For God's sake, sit down. Five minutes more and you'll have us finished."

Mr. Robinson came, with a shock, to himself, or rather out of himself into that sense of others which makes life as we know it. He looked down the room,

and before him surged wave on wave of smiling faces,
laughing faces, or faces merely baffled.  Laughter thun-
dered in his ears like the sea.  They thought him funny;
thought, at the best, that he was meaning to be funny,
at the worst that election excitement or strong liquor
had unhinged his mind.  Some faces in the room, and
many faces on the platform, stared at him appalled.

*"Sit down,"* hissed his agent in his ear, and, mechanically, he sat down.

Mechanically he listened, while the Chairman explained that Mr. Robinson, over-strained with his
week's exertions, was unable to continue speaking, but
that his place would be taken by his friend and sup-
porter Mr. Thompson.  Mr. Thompson stepped forward and began speaking.  What he said had a
familiar ring. . . .

Mr. Robinson leant forward.  He twitched the chairman by the sleeve.

"You were wrong about them," he whispered.
"They didn't want truth."

"You incredible ass," murmured the chairman.  Not
to wait until after polling day to get drunk, he meant.

# SOME PUBLIC MATTERS

# INCREASING DAILY

IT seems that the world has grown too full, and is daily growing fuller. For all the disastrous war which appeared to be emptying it, for all the falling birth-rate which ought to be keeping the numbers of our citizens down, we increase daily. Nothing we can do about it seems to avail. Probably another Black Death itself would not deplete but would replenish the earth. We cannot stay the monstrous multiplication of human beings who crawl on the face of the crowded globe.

The streets of towns are getting fuller; fuller of persons walking, persons standing, and vehicles to carry persons. The vehicles are not only more numerous, but more full. There was a time, before the great catastrophe which has so increased us, when we could walk about the streets with comparative ease, and when an omnibus could bear us along more rapidly than we could walk, instead of halting through the congested city at two miles an hour.

The country is getting fuller. There was a time when a country road was like a quiet brown stream, not a rushing, raging torrent, whose surface you may not see for the shrieking crafts which propel themselves along it. And this cannot be only due to the increase of motor vehicles, for in the old days the roads were not full even of pedestrians. You only· met one now and again.

Villages are getting fuller. Fuller of buildings; for those vile and meddlesome barbarians, County Councillors, those still more degraded Philistines, Urban District Councillors, have decreed that no village shall remain unspoiled, that houses shall spring up like mushrooms in hitherto virgin places, and that Towns shall be Planned.

Schools are getting fuller. I am told by parents that it is next door to impossible in these days to get their children admitted into any schools, even if their names have been entered years beforehand. The same with the universities. There must be more young people, or else more of them desire education, for I am told that the elementary schools also are now congested to bursting point.

Hospitals are getting fuller. There must be more invalids, or else more of them desire (strangely) to be nursed in institutions.

Railway stations at holiday season are getting fuller. I learn this from the press, which says—each August and each Easter—"Record Crowds at Waterloo, Paddington and Charing Cross. Scenes." And since the larger part of those who start arrive, seaside and other resorts are getting fuller, so that now hundreds of holiday-makers sleep on the sands. You may perhaps think that this exodus makes London, and the other cities whence these persons sally forth, emptier.

You are wrong. London, too, is fuller at holiday seasons than ever it was before. The overflow sleeps in the Parks and on Embankment benches.

Places of amusement are getting fuller. Restaurants and hotels are getting fuller. Abroad is getting fuller. The Italian Riviera, the Balearic isles, the coral islands of the South Seas—once pleasant, secluded retreats for the shy and unsociable—are all now congested, and scarcely repay a visit.

Shops are getting fuller. This, too, one learns from the press. During the sales, and before Christmas, one reads again and again of "Record Crowds. Scenes." I have been less fortunate than these journalists in never having witnessed a "scene," either at a railway station or in a shop, but the crowds I have certainly observed.

Homes are getting fuller. Yes; in spite of all this going forth for amusement, travel, and to make scenes, homes are getting fuller. They are more over-crowded than ever; or, anyhow, one hears more about it.

Prisons are getting fuller. More persons are incarcerated, but this does not leave fewer of them at large. The same with lunatic asylums.

There are more of almost every kind of person. More men, more women, more politicians, more writers, more workers, more workless, more burglars, more persons selling matches. The air is fuller, and the earth, and the water under the earth.

And yet every now and then I read in the public press two strange complaints. It seems that there are two receptacles for human life which are not fuller, but rather less full. These are churches and cradles. "Why are our churches empty?" someone will write every now and then to inquire. And the empty cradle has become a slogan. These phrases have a strange, soothing sound in these congested days. Are churches and cradles indeed empty? If they are, it is obvious that some redistribution of human beings is called for. Into churches and cradles should be poured some of the overflow which chokes the world outside them. I have even heard that there are too few clergymen, though too many of every other kind of person. Why not turn some of the politicians, novelists, burglars, or matchsellers into clergymen? Why not herd some of the Record Crowds from street, station, shop, and school into the churches, so that journalists should cry "Scenes" here too? Why not put some of the apparently abounding infants one sees in parks, streets, and perambulators into the cradles? In a congested world, why should any complaint of emptiness be allowed to pass unremedied?

But, even were this attempt at re-distribution accomplished, I doubt, from analogous experience, whether it would diminish the fullness elsewhere. It would probably increase it. It always does. Fill churches and cradles never so full, and you shall have a fuller world outside them also. It will merely mean that no empty place will be left us on the earth's face, not so much as a cradle. There is no solution here.

There is probably no solution anywhere. Neither

have we reason to suppose that death will relieve our congestion, for it is certain that the Other Countries, too, get fuller. Their denizens are, doubtless, grumbling about it, even as we: but at least they must perceive the reason of it. Whereas in our case there seems to be no reason; it is merely one of those lunatic and irrational facts with which nature, life, and the world abound. Ours not to reason why. We must just put up with it.

But one would like to know where it will all end.

## THE PRESS AND THE PUBLIC

THE life of the editor of a newspaper is, it must be supposed, a continual process of selection. Consider, for instance, those amazing (and amazed) periodicals which bloom (unlike the evening primrose) from ten each morning until nightfall, putting forth every two hours or so a fresh flower. Consider the editor, the news editor and the staff of these journals confronted throughout each day by the problem— "Which among to-day's occurrences shall we record? Which shall form the staple of our paper? Which shall be blazoned forth in placards by the wayside? Which, in fact, shall be to-day our Feature?" So they make their selection. Until about lunch-time their minds dwell on horses, their matutinal news is mainly concerned with the competitions of these animals one with another at equine sports and pastimes. Games played with balls also often occupy their morning thoughts; for they believe, very truly, that their readers find pleasure in learning who has excelled in these games. But, about noon-tide, what time their City Lunch Special, or whatever it may be called, makes ready to burgeon forth, news-editors seem to turn to the wider world; and, from then until their final edition brings the day's happenings to a close, they occupy themselves in setting down what they regard as News. I do not know whether they consider first what interests themselves or what they conceive will interest their readers. But, however they do it, they appear, oddly enough, to have arrived somehow at a kind of general convention on the matter. Perhaps the queerest thing about our queer press is the general resemblance of the contents of one newspaper to the contents of another. It would seem as if all editors leapt every day to approximately the same conclusions as to the desires of humanity for information about the world's happenings.

As to the matter thus arbitrarily selected for presentation, many interesting questions rise. Space being limited, I cannot here ask them all, nor, indeed, answer any. But I ask two. At which sections of the reading public are the various items aimed? And do they hit or miss? How much insight, that is, has the journalist into the minds of his fellow-creatures?

There is, of course, some news of almost universal interest, which finds a response in nearly every breast. Of such a kind are informations concerning peace and war, earthquakes, railway accidents, and strikes, weather, food, and Wimbledon. Of such a kind, too, is—"Mare with Rabies Bites Five Cows," and such thrilling fragments from the world of marvels. Then there is the news meant for a section only—political and parliamentary news, foreign news, news of Royal Persons, books or plays, the public utterances of those who publicly utter, and so forth.

But for what section of readers are such statements

as this, that you may see any day in almost any paper?
"Anne Jones, an old woman of ninety, died at Llanilar
last week. Though bedridden, her intellect was still
keen." It would be interesting to know if any reader
is stirred by this, or so much as says "fancy" to it.
Does it, perhaps, interest other old persons, as yet un-
deceased? But even they can scarcely think it strange,
or more than very slightly sad. Old age must come:
old women do die: that is incontrovertible. Anne
Jones remains a problem to me. Frankly, I believe her
to be a journalistic miss. I do not think she reaches
any mark.

But I may be wrong. For at least the journalist has
tradition on his side. I was reading the other day one
of the irregularly issued news sheets of the year 1669,
and came on the following: "A certain Rotcheller, called
Isaack Chapron, aged eighty-two years, having travelled
sixty years through the four parts of the world, is deceased, having ten days before his death abjured his
religion in the church of the Jesuits." Here is Anne
Jones, a little amplified and adorned, but still, merely
an old man deceased. So perhaps there has always been
a public which likes to read of deaths, even the deaths
in bed of the old.

But why weddings? Are weddings ever interesting,
except to the principals and their friends? Is it possible that there are those who read with pleasure of the
marriages of those unknown to them? And, if so,
why? These functions lack even the interest of universal occurrence; they do not happen to quite every-

body, and they do happen to so many as to miss the interest of singularity. Are they, indeed, read? And are there any readers found to care that the bride wore white tulle and the bridesmaids pink gauze, or whatever brides and bridesmaids do wear on such occasions?

Of divorces I will not here speak. I can only presume that those, if any, who like to read of the union of perfect strangers read also with interest of the union's severance. The human mind is, in many cases, a fathomless pit of sentimental sympathies, which it is not for the cold and hard, such as you and I, to probe. Doubtless all these things find a happy home in some eager breast.

Sometimes, indeed often, the press seems to agree that some item in the day's news is of such enthralling interest, so very amazing, that it must usurp all the placards and nearly all the front page of every paper. In this category journalists place crime, and more particularly murder. "So-and-so in the Dock," they will cry. "Amazing Statements"—and in detail will follow the story, which only very occasionally has elements of interest, and is more often commonplace, crude and flat, amazing only to those very easily amazed. Human drama, doubtless, and probably melodrama, but with no intrinsic interest. To sophisticated minds, such stories, thus set forth, are merely a bore; to the fastidious and sensitive they are also a horror and a tragedy. To open one's paper and come on them is like stumbling into a slaughter yard, or into a home for very dull criminal lunatics. To simpler or robuster souls, whose demands are small, the perusal of such matter may be a pleasure. The journalists may be right. They cater mainly, after all, for the simple and the robust. They are catering, in this matter, further, for the streak of brutality which is in the primitive human mind, and which has, ever since we cumbered the earth, delighted in torture, horror, and death—that brutality which sent our ancestors eagerly to watch executions, which sends crowds even now to get as near to an execution as may be, and which loves, if it cannot witness horrors, to read of them. News editors, knowing well that this delight in horror exists, proceed to feed it with anything they can lay their hands on. Murder, suicide, the dismembering of corpses, any grim, stupidly crude thing does. They serve it up, hot and spiced, to tickle the palates of the gourmets, and advertise their day's menu with a flourish.

It is interesting to speculate what proportion of newspaper readers are bored by this police-court material, and in what proportion it meets a demand. Presumably journalists have thus speculated, and made their decision. They may be right. We are a simple people, with a simple taste in reading matter. Many of us like to read of others being murdered, cut up, and put away in hen-houses or trunks. More will read these tales if they are there, as they will read anything else. Newspapers have us in the hollow of their hands, out of which we meekly eat; we are not particular. All we want (most of us) is a nice piece of reading as we go home from work in the bus or train.

We do not demand tales of crime—any other exciting story does for us. But the purveyors of news have decided that we are to have these things, in as large doses as possible. Warm human life-stuff: that is what the news editor (himself, probably, a simple fellow) likes to give us. The same quality perhaps makes him an affectionate husband and father. It does not make him, for those who care little for warm human life-stuff, an interesting or entertaining selector of the world's news. But he may well retort that such should not read the penny press, and that, if they do, they can very easily omit such material as they do not care for.

And, no doubt, he is quite right. Anyhow he has always been the same. The earliest news sheets were full of the same kind of sensational drama—wives poisoning their husbands, parents butchering children, and what not. The public taste has always been thus diagnosed, whether accurately or not.

But of one thing I am sure. Most newspaper readers like leading articles. For these curious effusions sum up our incoherent thoughts for us and give them shape—whether the same shape as the leader writer's or one widely different, called into being by opposition. Some people can only maintain themselves in what they consider sound political principles by regularly reading opposition leaders. Before the leaders of the papers with which they are in agreement, their faith falters and dims; it looks so weak, so improbable, put like that. . . .

But more people prefer to see their own thoughts

about events set out for them in print; it is nearly as satisfactory as having written them themselves, and how much less trouble!

I close with a suggestion. I would urge the newspaper world to try the experiment of leaving out most of what they at present publish, of publishing much of what they at present leave out, and see if the result is not accepted meekly by the public and consumed with unquestioning relish. For we are wonderfully tamed.

## ON CERTAIN TRAFFICS

IT is well known that most traffic is wrong, and needs to be suppressed. The very word has an evil connotation. "Often," says the dictionary, "used in a sinister sense." Yes, indeed. The League of Nations knows this, and devotes much of its time and many of its best committees to a discussion of various forms of traffic and how to stop them. There is (unfortunately) the cocaine traffic, the opium traffic, the white slave traffic, the black slave traffic, the traffic in women and children, traffic in souls, and (worse than them all) the traffic in the streets. There is also the Ministry of Traffic (though it may call itself, euphemistically, Transport), which probably directs all these.

I do not quite know at what point honest trade becomes traffic, but, when it has done so, the only thing is to suppress it. The suppression of traffic—the two words are so connected that they trip off the tongue together. Unfortunately the worst and most deadly of the traffics, street or motor traffic, is not suppressed at all, but encouraged. No other traffic—no, not the opium traffic—takes so much human life. Not that this is the worst count against motor traffic, for, after all, man must die somehow, and why not thus, unless he dislikes being taken so suddenly, unhouseled, disappointed, unaneled, and he has no excuse for venturing into the public roads nowadays in this state. No; a worse crime of the motor traffic than its toll of human life is its toll of human minds. Not the cocaine traffic itself has so much insanity to its credit. Daily our asylums are being filled with certified patients, our cities with uncertified maniacs, all driven mad with the authentic din of hell. Even worse than this is the toll of human souls. Not the white slave traffic itself, not the very traffic in souls, has so many lost creatures to its credit. The fiery angers, the black disgust and despair, that wreck the souls of those who walk on country roads vainly seeking peace, and those who live perforce in country villages, is perhaps the deadliest count against this blackest of traffics.

Yet it is not suppressed. No government is brave enough to say that these infernal machines must not, any more than trains do, run along public roads, but must, if they would run at all, make for themselves separate ways, as trains did. No: governments too have cars, and are involved, soul and body, in this fearful traffic.

Enough. I must not dwell further on the obscene thing. My pen ran on. It always does, when I refer to this subject. I feel like the prophet Jeremiah about it—denunciatory. Let us turn to another and more harmless traffic—the traffic in literature. Perhaps traffic may be considered by some too harsh a name for this trade. But, by now, the writing habit has surely become a vice. And one foresees that, like other agreeable vices, it will probably soon be suppressed by a paternal government. The literature traffic may well, like the cocaine traffic, and unlike worse traffics, be driven underground, to be hunted down by Scotland Yard. Houses, shops, publishing and printing works, may be raided for books, newspapers, and other forms of the printed word, and we shall have the intriguing spectacle of literature fiends being haled before the law and sentenced for their misdemeanours. I am no advocate of any of the tyrannies of impertinent and bureaucratic governments; I am a libertarian and an individualist; in my view all men should be free to practise even their vices, until these vices interfere with the well-being of their neighbours; my main objection to that in some ways fairly innocuous assembly, the two Houses of Parliament, is their impudent tampering with our individual and personal liberties. But, if we are not to be allowed to drug as we please, to drink as we please, to dress, behave, spend our money, and travel as we please, if these tyrannies are to be exercised over us by these loquacious and inquisitive minions whom we place in authority over us, let them at least interfere to some good purpose, and check those vices which most need it. And since we can trust no government to discriminate between good and bad in literature, or indeed in anything else, their only safe way would be to forbid all printed output. Signor Mussolini of Italy sets us an example of literary suppression thoroughly ill done; he forbids only so much of the contemporary press as does not please him. This, the method pursued by ourselves and all the belligerent countries during the recent European war, is not a good one, since governments have their own rather peculiar standards of taste, and what pleases them is not, as a rule, good literature, nor what displeases them bad. No, the only method of suppression fit for governments is the wholesale method. And, much as I personally should regret this, its results would be not in all ways displeasing. Imagine, for instance, waking each morning to a world without newspapers. What a quiet, provincial little world, each corner of it filled with only the hum of its own busy doings, each teacup turbulent with its own storms. The chief events of each day might be posted in public places, or broadcasted, so that we might, if we cared to, know how the world was getting on. But no more printed pages crackling at our breakfast tables with foolish tales of suicide, murder, reparations, and vanishing lapwings (I wish that lapwing would vanish and have done), the last fall from his horse of a royal prince, the last speech of a politician about how his party is the best party, the last vulgar wrangle in Parliament, the last inept utterances of critics about inept plays and books. No more leading articles; no more evening papers. We shall walk the streets without being confronted each moment with placards announcing Gallops and Naps; we shall feel the world a quieter, duller, less horsey place. We shall return to the pleasant ignorance of our remoter ancestors, who did so well without these informations. So much for jour-

nalism. (Though for my part, I may as well say at
once, I should miss it a good deal.) As to other
reading matter—(and, if you come to that, as to journalism too, I suppose)—you may say that it does not
hurt us, or need suppression, for we need not read it.
Very true. And this is true also of cocaine, which does
not hurt us either for we need not eat it (or inject
it, or sniff it up, or whatever one does with cocaine).
Myself I should say this about most of the world's
produce—perhaps all except motor traffic, which is an
obviously inescapable nuisance, to which we cannot
shut our eyes or ears. All I say is that, logically, if
you suppress anything, you ought to suppress everything, including literature. Speaking not only as an
individualist and a libertarian, but as a trader in the
literature traffic, I of course am all against literary
suppression. Personally I would urge the government,
if they must suppress anything, to suppress smallpox,
which they, oddly, show no signs of wishing to do; or
Sheffield, or Glasgow, or, as I suggested, motor traffic,
or public monuments, or cocks that crow in the small
hours, or the Houses of Parliament. Books are not
noxious, or violent, or even audible. They cannot hurt
those who do not open them. They, like the
drama, are harmless nuisances. They will, in most
cases, bore you if you read them just as drama may
bore you if you see it, but there is no call to do either.
And—for I do not wish to be wholesale—some books,
as we all know, are even worth reading, just as some
plays are worth seeing. Some of the literature pro-

duced by humanity has been good literature. Beauty
has been produced, and laughter, and comedy, and tragedy, and terror, and good readable tales in plenty, and
poetry, and criticism, and drama. There have always
been these things in the literature of all times, but far
too rarely. For the most part, the written word has
always been rather insipid, pointless, and mediocre—
indifferent stuff. For that matter, the bulk of produc-
tion in all spheres, whether artistic, scientific, utilitarian,
human, or any other, has been on a lowish level. What
can one expect? Literature is no worse than anything
else. Look at medical science. Look at houses. Look
at education. Look at British Empire exhibitions.
Look at clothes. Look at religions. Look at babies.
Look, if you like, at the whole animal world, human
and other. We are but indifferent creatures, mostly,
and so most of our produce is indifferent stuff too.
Do not blame us for that. For very well suited to us
it mostly is. For my part, I enjoy it very much. If
all literature were good literature, the circulating libraries might as well close down. The remarkable thing
is that we should be able to produce any literature at all.
I am always struck afresh by the surprising comparative cleverness of humanity whenever I visit the Zoo,
and consider the lack of intellectual output of these
our fellow-creatures, so like in many ways to ourselves.
How have we risen to our present level of intelligence,
of productiveness? We are very certainly the cleverest
of the creatures, and the expression of ideas with pen
on paper is a surprising achievement. Far be it from

me to advocate its suppression. I am merely prophesy-ing, and wondering why it has not yet occurred. It seems, according to precedent, more than time that governments laid to their hands and did something about it. Only I do hope that they will deal with worse traffics first.

## BEDS AND 'OMES

WE each had our own sad business there; what mine was matters not except to myself. And we each of us had, while waiting for our cases to come on, our compensating and illuminating vision of the Law at work on the cases of others. We had none of us, I think, done very wrong. The worst moral offender was a seller of under-weight coal. The crimes of the rest of us might be called peccadilloes—bicycling on footpaths or without lights, motoring too fast, or unlawfully permitting certain dogs to be at large without being efficiently muzzled as required by the Muzzling and Control of Dogs Order, 1919. These things will happen in the best regulated lives. The chief interest of the cases (except for an occasional acrimonious dispute between defendant and policeman) was the recital by the policeman of what each offender had said at the moment of conviction of crime.

"Defendant said he was not on the footpath and there was no footpath and a van was occupying the whole road and we might as well live in Berlin."

A mistake it had been, to say all that.

"Defendant said she was very sorry, but the dog must have escaped over the gate or through a hole in the hedge."

That was more the sort of thing to say. Defendant,

on hearing her words repeated by the constable in a
loud and monotonous recitative, congratulated herself
that she had said no worse.

We were all treated firmly but not unkindly. None
of us were hectored or bullied, though a cyclist fined
five shillings for riding without lights was told grimly,
and doubtless inaccurately, by the Bench that he was
lucky, it might have been a hundred pounds.

But then a change came over the manner of the
Court. There was a hustling at a side door, and from
an inner room a little old man was brought forth.
A grey, unshaven little old man, with earth-coloured
clothes and the quick, side-long look of the gipsy. A
stout and dignified policeman stood in the box and
swore before Almighty God that defendant had arrived in the town one night drunk and disorderly, and
had inquired at the Police Station for a bed. . . .

"Have you anything to say?" the defendant was
asked, quite fairly and politely.

"No, sir; except, sir, that there's not a word of
truth in anything that gentleman's been saying about
me."

"Well, do you wish to go into the box and make
a statement on oath?"

"Just as you like, sir. It's all one to me. I'd as
soon make my statement from here. I speak the
truth wherever I am, and whether I'm on oath or not."

So he made his statement.

The chief thing that emerged was that he hadn't
been drunk; not at all. On arriving in the town from

somewhere else he had only had a glass of beer at
the Railway Tavern, then two more up in the town
at the White Hart, then a pint and a half at the Saracen
—and how could he be drunk on that? He had then
gone to the Police Station and asked if they had
a bed.

"The gentleman there ought to have asked me to
come in and sit down while he inquired. He ought to
have said . . ."

"Never mind what he ought to have said."

The Inspector rose up and addressed the Bench.

"I ought to say that we've 'ad warnings about this
defendant from all over the country. He's not at all
an estimable character; judging by his habits. We've
been told that he's slept rough for years. It's years
since he slept in a bed."

That was all the warning. But it was enough. Defendant's head drooped guiltily; the Justices looked
stern, the Constabulary severe and disdainful.

"I never get drunk, sir," pleaded defendant, picking up courage even in the face of this slur on his
character. "I've worked on and off on Mr. Piggot's
farm for years; he wouldn't have kept me if I'd got
drunk. Mr. Piggot is in court, sir."

"Have you anything to say about this man, Mr.
Piggot?" (No longer "the defendant"; he slept rough,
therefore he was now "this man.")

Mr. Piggot rose in his place.

"It's quite true, sir, that he's a rough sleeper. Hasn't
slept in a bed since I've known him."

That settled the case.

"Seven days," said the Bench.

"Thank you, sir," said defendant, and shuffled meekly away, to sleep in a bed at last.

He left me musing on the strange standards by which society passes judgment on the individual. Sleeping in a bed—it is, apparently, of immense importance. Against those who sleep, from choice or necessity, elsewhere society feels righteously hostile. It is not done. It is disorderly, anarchical. We have decided that the periods of rest which divide day from day shall be spent, as a matter of regular routine, on mattresses, between sheets and blankets. Only a war, or an exploring expedition, or a boy-scout outing, or other social and conscious campings out, can excuse departure from this habit. To be found sleeping in a public place is like being found without visible means of support—an indictable offence. Further, it is an indication of sin. "He sleeps rough"—therefore he is, doubtless, a thief, a drunkard, and a liar. There seems no reason why similar evidence should not be brought in a contrary sense to prove a man's worth.

"Have you anything to say about the defendant, witness?"

"Only, sir, that he sleeps very comfortably at nights, with an eiderdown and a hot bottle and tea when he is called. He's not slept out of bed since I've known him."

"Very good. Defendant is discharged."

He sleeps soft; he must be an honest and good man.

His taste runs on normal lines in the matter of nocturnal habits, and he has the means to gratify it. Acquitted, with the esteem of the Court. He is not a perverse vagrant, who lies curled up like an animal in a ditch or field with the open sky above him. Against such the law has declared war. Not long since it was the stocks and branding iron.

I had once to pass the night at a railway station, having missed a late train home. I wanted, when tired of exploring the neighbouring streets, to sit in the ladies' waiting-room. It was locked, and only unlocked for me under protest.

"If we were to keep the rooms unlocked at nights," I was told, "we should have all the ladies without 'omes coming in. That wouldn't be very nice. . . ."

All the ladies without 'omes. Pathetic, tragic picture. That night I was myself one of them, and knew exactly how cold they were, how 'omeless, how forlorn and weary, comforted only by the coffee stall at the corner of the street. Ladies without 'omes—gentlemen sleeping rough. Society has decreed that these ladies and gentlemen, on the chance nights when for some reason they do happen to want a bed or an 'ome, should be denied these. They have forfeited their right.

In the eternal war waged between society and the vagrant, the vagrant must always lose. But why should society add insult to injury by scorning and insulting the vagrant for his unusual tastes? Is not this a matter with which the Societies for Equal Citizenship might well concern themselves?

In the unhappy name of liberty let us be allowed to sleep precisely as we prefer. Beds are a taste, like another. So, for that matter, are 'omes. Why make a fetish of either?

It is interesting to speculate on the probable attitude of contemporary society towards St. Simon Stylites and other of the less comfortable good men and women of history.

"We've been warned against this man, sir. He sleeps on a pillar—very uncomfortable indeed, and most peculiar. Not at all an estimable character, judging by his habits. . . ."

SOME PRIVATE MATTERS

# TRAVELLING BY TRAIN

WHAT strange moving prisons are these, I reflected, in which we so often and so willingly
confine ourselves, abstracting our bodies, souls, and
spirits from the daily life we lead, enshrining ourselves in a remote and mystic detachment, enclosing
ourselves in a small, hurrying space, along with others
of our kind, never encountered before, never, God willing, to be encountered again. Fellow-prisoners for a
moment out of eternity; ships that pass in the night,
and that sometimes, but not as a rule, speak one another
in passing. . . .

*"Do you mind the window up?"*

*"Oh, no. Oh, no, indeed . . ."*

Oh, yes, I said within myself, I do mind the window up. If I had wished the window up, should I
not have put it up before? We have not got away
from lies, in this detached and flying cage that swings
beyond life's edge. Here, if anywhere, honesty should
be possible; therefore honesty is nowhere possible,
which is what I have always suspected.

*"Excuse me, you've dropped your stamp book. . . .
And these letters on the floor—are they yours?"*

*"Thank you."*

How kind, how kind. And how officious, and how
unreasoning. I threw the stamp book on the floor be-

cause it was finished; I dropped those empty envelopes
because I had extracted their contents and answered
them so far as was necessary. Had you looked a little more closely, had you been a little less kind, or a
little more ready to assume in me the normal amount
of wits, we should both have been spared trouble, you
the trouble of collecting waste paper from a dirty floor,
I the greater labour of saying thank you. But, all
the same, how kind. I am not kind like that. I let
people retrieve their own dropped possessions, assuming that, if they do not do so, they have, for one reason or another, wearied of them. Then, in case there
should be a stamp book, with perhaps a halfpenny stamp
left in it, or even more, I would linger after they were
got out (*alighted:* this is the railway companies' pretty
phrase) and collect it to my own advantage. As to
their dropped letters, what better thing can you do with
letters than to drop them? Such a habit, if cultivated,
will save you many a tedious hour of answering them.
Personally, I never answer letters but in trains; elsewhere there is always something better to do. Even
in trains there are better things to do; pull the win-
dows up and down, watch the landscape race by like a
galloping horse, pull the communication cord, or merely
sit, hypnotised into a drowsy peace, as you dash through
space. Or listen to the conversation of your fellows,
which reaches you only in curious, isolated fragments
from which you may or may not deduce the rest.

"*When I go through Denham I always think of
Dot. . . .*"

Strange! And yet, why not?

*"Yes; I always have to think of Dot when I pass Denham."*

There; she has said it again; it must be true. Perhaps Dot lives at Denham, or died there, or committed there some awful crime. The speaker, I infer, does not want to think of Dot, for *"I have to,"* she says. Perhaps Dot married the man loved by the speaker, and his name was Denham . . . or can it merely be that Dot and Denham both begin with D?

Anyhow, it starts in me a train of thought. When I pass Baker Street I have to think of Mr. Holmes. When I pass Stratford-on-Avon I have to think of William Shakespeare and Miss Corelli. When I go through Criccieth I have (how distressing) to think of erstwhile Prime Ministers. At Hatfield I like to think about the League of Nations; at Wembley of our Empire, Mr. Tex Austin, and the Prince of Wales in butter; at Glasgow of Members of Parliament, full of sound and fury; at Cambridge of Naps (I read often about these on newspaper placards, but I do not know what they are), and when my train runs into Waterloo I have to think of Wellington and poor Napoleon. It is all very interesting. But, all the same, I do not much care about having to think in trains; trains should not be trains of thought; one can think (after a fashion) anywhere; trains are set apart, in my opinion, for better occupations. Mystic, swinging, rumbling rooms, hurtling their little prisoners from one portion of the busy earth to another—in them, if anywhere, we should enjoy peace and nothingness, slung thus above earth, between time and time. We should not, I reflected, meditating on this subject, even have to think of Dot.

Instead of doing so, I began to ruminate on the various things which have happened to me in trains. How once I saw a baby being sick; how at other times there have been hens in baskets, and often a dog. How a young Hungarian once told me he was about to take his life and I knew not what to say, but that it seemed to me a pity. How I have been enclosed alone with murderers and with lunatics, who nevertheless restrained themselves, even in tunnels, from doing me damage. How mercifully I have been preserved, amid all the perils of locomotion, and brought safely to my destinations. . . . Never have I had even the faintest pretext for pulling that tempting cord. One day I shall do it, and pay the price contentedly. To bring a train to a standstill; to set officials running hither and thither, all agog for sensation; it is cheap at the price. Cheaper than spitting, which costs forty shillings (first time) and surely is not worth it.

It gives food for thought, this tariff of expensive amusements which may be purchased in trains. One turns the money in one's pocket; in fancy one spends it. . . .

But here we are. One more romantic journey is over. When I get to Beaconsfield I have to think of primroses . . . no, the time for thinking is past; I have to get out.

# ON LIVING LIFE TO THE FULL

I READ the phrase (not for the first time, for, in slightly different wordings, I seem to have been reading it all my life) in my Sunday morning paper, under the heading "Sayings of the Week." It had been said or written by someone—I think a novelist —in the course of the week, and the *Observer* had been struck by its truth, or perhaps by its absence of truth, and had selected it for quotation, along with other noteworthy remarks made by public characters. (I was once in that column myself, but on the strength of something I had never said, so possibly the novelist had not said this, either.) Anyhow, the remark, whoever made it, set me thinking. "The only real crime," it ran, "is not to live life to the full."

With mixed feelings I meditated on this. First, I confess I experienced some degree of satisfaction in reflecting that, if this were indeed so, my life had been more innocent than I thought. To be sure, I had at every moment in it, committed the only real crime; but then, I had committed no others; all those actions which had lain on my conscience need not have burdened it at all, for they were not real crimes. Defrauding the widow and the orphan, ravishing the poor, taking human life or the wives of others, worshipping idols, defrauding railway companies, tax collectors and penny-in-the-slot machines, closing right-of-way footpaths, running down pedestrians with cars, killing dogs, defacing landscape with advertisements, forging cheques, paying bills with bad coins, insulting grey heads and despising infants, smoking in non-smokers, taking babes by train, cheating at rummy, repeating scandal, annexing land, forcing elections on a patient people—all these that I had thought were crimes (I am not meaning to imply, by the way, that I have committed them all) were not real crimes, but only amiable peccadilloes. This was cheering. And it was consoling also to reflect that, though I had indeed committed all day and every day, through countless years, the only real crime, so had everyone else. Its commission is inevitable. Life may be prodigious, enormous, morbidly distended, but never can it be quite full. I take "full" to mean full of energies, activities, deeds, emotions. Of course, it is always full of something, if only of inertia, but one must, I suppose, attribute some meaning to the phrase as used, and I take it that its user meant something more active and exciting than that.

My life, then, began to look to me a sadly criminal affair. All the things I had left undone crowded up before my accusing conscience. I had not played mah-jong, dyed the hair, worshipped in a Plymouth Brothers' chapel or a Jewish synagogue, visited the South Seas, the Zoo aquarium, Montmartre, Sheffield, Los Angeles, or Baham, injected cocaine, made a bead purse or a will, won money on a horse, found oil or gold, captured a flea, learnt Hebrew, Russian, American, or Chinese, suffered an operation (excepting only on the teeth), stood for Parliament, got married, adopted a child or a pet monkey, taken the veil. . . . In the light of all the life I had not lived, the life I had lived, which used to look to me enough, or even too much, faded to insignificance. Why, I reflected with shame, I had not even written a play, taken Kruschen salts, or lectured in America.

I must, I thought, see about this. I must not go on daily committing the only real crime. All the authorities seemed to be agreed about the desirability of fullness—even the Bible, I was sure, said it somewhere—so they must be right. I will, I thought, endeavour to live one crimeless day, even should it be my last. I will begin it early and cause to be brought to me in bed coffee, chocolate, and tea. Thus sustained, I shall rise and go out before breakfast, and run round Hyde Park, knocking down a policeman, addressing to a gentleman or two unsolicited attentions, picking the dahlias, stoning the squirrels, and kidnapping an infant from its perambulator. I shall return home (infant with me, for it is time I became a mother, since I have heard that no woman's life is really full without the patter of tiny feet and the embrace of little arms) and have breakfast to the full, which is the kind you get in Scotland and on liners—grapefruit, porridge, cereals, tea, coffee, ham, eggs, kidneys, haddock, herring, sole, kedgeree, marmalade, honey, jam, butter, toast, scones. Having consumed this to the full, I shall

smoke five cigarettes and make out a cheque to self
for all my remaining bank balance. I shall call at the
bank on my way to the full life of London, which
cannot be lived with empty pockets.

But the morning, indeed the whole day, is so full
of possibilities of amplitude that I do not feel able
to make a plan for it; I must trust to the inspiration
of the moment. I do not know whether I shall go to
Wembley (where life is very full indeed, particularly
in the Amusements Park) or to Selfridge's, where it
is, in its way, even fuller, or visit an opium den in
Limehouse, or a Christian Science Hall, or Scotland
Yard with a confession of murder, or Downing Street
disguised as a foreign ambassador. Or I might call
on some Bishop, and ask him what he thinks about
the Fall. . . .

I do not know where I shall lunch, whether at the
Ritz, in Greek Street, or at a Lyons' soda fountain,
where I can have a mixed fruit sundae, a parfait, a
frappé, a shake, an ice cream soda, and a phosphate,
all at once. After lunch, I may or may not have a
trip in an aeroplane, a cocaine orgy, a matinée, a
scene in the street with the police or in the House
of Commons with the usher. I do not know which
would be the fullest. Whichever I do, there will be
time after it to get out of London; the full life must
include the country life, so I will take a train somewhere; it does not matter where, so long as I enrich
the journey by pulling the communication cord and
informing the guard that my fellow-traveller is a dan-

gerous lunatic. Having arrived in the country, I must take a country walk, and, I suppose, pluck whatever flowers are at the moment blowing. It will be advisable to go through private grounds, and also to call at at least one house and inform the owner that I know all and that my price for not mentioning it is ten pounds down. If I get away before the police are summoned, I shall visit the local church, attend evensong, and during it rise to protest against the manner of its conduct, as being too high, low, or broad. That is to say, if it is a low church, I shall pose as a Kensitite and protest against its scandalous ritualism; if it is high, I shall be Anglo-Catholic, and demand more candles, incense, confession, and meditation; if it is broad, I shall be modernist, and cry out against its obscurantism. Whichever is the case, I shall live a full life before being ejected from the church.

Having thus lived, I suppose I shall return to London, where, they say, life by night is fuller than in the country. A full night life in London begins, of course, with dinner, and proceeds with several theatres in succession; a few minutes in each will suffice, but one must not fail, during at least one of them, to pay a visit, however brief, to the dressing-room of some popular and beautiful actor. If he prove unwelcoming, *tant pis;* one must procure someone else as supper companion and as dancing partner at one's night club.

I will refrain from following this splendid, this prodigious night, in detail; it might not be proper, since it should include orgies of all descriptions. To complete the circle of my twenty-four hours, I suppose it must continue until morning, since full livers can scarcely waste time in mere sleep. I must end it with an hour or so of some kind of work, for every full life should contain this unpleasing ingredient. Then, with the morning, wearied but proud, I shall creep to my bed and sleep, I hope, the dreamless sleep of a good conscience.

Thus I mused; as we all weave day-dreams for ourselves which well we know will never be fulfilled. But even so, even granted my day and night as I have described them, would they pass the test? Are they full enough? Though to me they look so full, it is possible that to other and fuller livers they may appear pale, attenuated and empty. After all, they are full of omissions; they do not include standing for Parliament, seeing a hanging or a bus accident, visiting an asylum or the Zoo. They include, in fact, scarcely anything; they do but touch the fringes of Life.

We may not, I reflected, judge one another. For one man's fullness is another's emptiness, and who shall be the condemner of his brother's crime?

Thus meditating, I dismissed this preposterous Sayings of the Week with a snap of the fingers. After all, we could every one of us invent a score of crimes as bad as that, and label them as the only real one, straight off. The only real crime I might say, is not to keep a dog, not to have a gramophone, not to wear the hair shingled. . . .

I care not for these arbitrary crime-makers. I can and will make a dozen real crimes to their one. And I will try and persuade the Sayings editor of the *Observer* to put them all in.

# ALONE

TO be idle and alone—here are two agreeable things. The first is easy; anyone can be idle, provided he is willing to endure the consequent penury. The second is more difficult and by no means always to be attained in this world of humanity, of the affections, of friendship, of family life, of Personally Conducted Tours. Yet, if you would have complete idleness, you must be alone. You will find, in the end, that there is only one person whose company entails no effort whatsoever. Only one person with whom, on a holiday, you need make no plans, discuss no arrangements, share no sandwiches, quarrel over no maps, lie in bed of a morning as long as you please, make no conversation and no sacrifices. Only one person with whom you need not trouble to keep your temper, whose taste in amusements and occupations is entirely as good as your own, whose opinion as to which road to take is as accurate as yours, who gets tired of walking or of sitting still at the same moment as you get tired yourself. However dull a person you may be, you will be good company to yourself. However good, entertaining, and beloved other company may be, be sure it will have its faults. Even if the worst of these should be wanting the map when you want it yourself, still, this is a bad fault.

There may, of course, be no question of maps on

a holiday. A holiday may be spent at home, the other occupants of the home having been sent away, with or without maps. But this kind of holiday is often more difficult to arrange. And people come to the door. They will not, if you are both cunning and firm, get beyond the door; but still, it is disquieting to have the bell ringing. The best plan is to put some deterrent notice on your front door, such as "Home for Dangerous Mental Cases. Do not irritate them." But, whatever precautions you may take, you will be safer in a place where you are not already known.

Besides, it is more amusing to be away. The British and the gypsies, alone among mankind, have that no-madic strain in them which makes them never so happy as when they are travelling abroad. To be at once abroad and alone—this is true felicity. It would be the truest felicity of all to discover a place where others of one's race, and potentially therefore of one's acquaintance, did not congregate; but this may not be, for Britons go everywhere. They share with the Sappers the motto *Ubique*. Go whither you will, to the highest peak of Everest, the hottest desert of Africa, the coolest ice-floe round the Poles, the remotest isle of the Pacific, and there you will find Britons. "De chacune des Touamotou, des Nouvelles Hebrides, et des Bahamas, une Anglaise en chandail jaillissait au moindre appel!" Go whither you will, and before you start be sure that someone will say to you—"Look out for my friends the Andersons; they are staying there. . . ."

What, having looked out for and perceived the Andersons, you are then to do to them, what they to you, these kindly and unthinking conversationalists do not state. Presumably you are to accost them. You are to say—"I think you know the Browns." They will either lose their heads and own that this is the case, or they will retain their presence of mind and deny it, saying that you must have confused them with someone else of the same name. If they own to the Browns, you say (I presume), "So do I"—unless you, in your turn, have the presence of mind to reply, "Well, *I* don't." Let us suppose that you have lost your nerve and owned to the Browns. What a link is here! You will both have to spend the rest of your time in this place loosening it. It is a wiser plan to look out for the Andersons, as requested, and, having perceived and located them, to turn your backs to them whenever you meet, and put down a false or indecipherable name in the inn register, lest they too should have been bidden to look out for you. For this, too, is perpetrated— "I will write to them about you."

What is the meaning of these apparently inexplicable outrages? Do those who commit them really themselves enjoy meeting and having to talk to strangers on a holiday, on the ground that both know the same person or persons in England? It can scarcely be. Is the attack, then, the outcome of some secret and malevolent envy? Do these persons think, scarcely knowing that they think it, "You and the Andersons will be away for a holiday, and I shall not; but at least I will do some small thing to mar the perfection of your holiday and theirs"? Who can say! The recesses of the human heart are dark and strange.

Rather would I attribute these curious outbreaks to more innocent and kindly motives, to the natural gregariousness of human kind, to the instinct which makes many of them at all times say, "Let us get together. Let us not be alone for a moment. Let us assemble together to play, to eat, to talk, to pray, to read"— for I have even known those who have started or joined what they call *reading-circles,* preferring to read whatever they are reading in company with others to reading it alone. It is the same sociable instinct which made the explorer Stanley, meeting the explorer Livingstone wandering in the desert heart of Africa, pause and say, "Dr. Livingstone, I presume," instead of passing by with a nod, which would have been so much less trouble. Let us charitably attribute all these attempts to bring others together to this instinct, which perhaps dates from primeval days when to be alone in the jungle was even less safe than to be together there.

Be that as it may, you can, while abroad, with a little cunning, resolution, and skill, avoid both the friends of others and (although this is more difficult) your own—unless you go to Cornwall in August, or the Riviera in spring, which is merely asking for it, and you deserve all you get. In August, it is not a bad plan to try London. You will not be alone; you will still be thronged around with those slow-moving street crowds who always appear to be either following a hearse, or crippled with rheumatism, so halting and deliberate is their gait; but you will not have to speak to them, and the odds are that those of them whom you know will either be away, or, if in London, be having a holiday too.

Anyhow, and wherever we go, let us endeavour at intervals to be both idle and alone, remembering that

> Two paradises are in one
> To dwell in paradise alone.

# ROMANCE

ROMANCE—that queer, elusive, heady state of mental intoxication—depends for its existence on two co-operating factors, the drink and the drinker. Almost any tipple, however apparently "soft," may to some particular tippler, assume suddenly the properties of fermented liquor, and go to the head or the heart, producing that delicious thrill of excitement, strangeness and wonder that we call romance. You may be assaulted by romance in the squalid and noisy streets of some vile industrial town, and such streets suddenly will stir with the beat of strange wings, becoming mystic lanes of beauty, terror, ghosts, or gods. But more probably not. "The angels keep their ancient places; turn but a stone and start a wing"—this may occur even if the stone pave a Manchester street; but it occurs more often elsewhere. Strangeness, loveliness, foreignness, wonder—these qualities may strike on the soul in any place (romance strikes Mr. Rudyard Kipling's soul, he once said, in railway stations, when the 9.15 train clatters in), but in some soils, some places, they are inherent, needing only the minimum of co-operation in the beholding mind. Even so, the mind has to do its share. We are not always susceptible. It is possible to stand, say, on the green rampart of an incredibly ancient British fosse that circles a little old

Wiltshire hamlet, looking on those mighty stones which our pre-historic forefathers had such a morbid passion for setting on end, and to feel nothing beyond "How interesting it is. How remarkably long ago. . . ." And it is possible, the next moment, to be flooded and submerged with mystery and romance, to discern everywhere our woaded fathers hauling at giant stones, celebrating orgies round those monstrous altars to their fearful gods, holding Roman and Saxon foes at bay from those green ramparts . . . or, merely, to be drowned in the sunlit sense of the little old lichened village dreaming away the centuries in its prehistoric cup. Then the downs will be radiant like green flame, the larks twitter their high, sweet notes like tunes from elfin spinets, the globe, turning in blue space, be as a flickering dream, under the spell of that intoxication that has descended on the dizzied soul. The spirit bloweth where it listeth; any hour may flame into a magic hour, any place lilt with the chime of fairy bells.

Yet romance is not entirely a casual and uninvited visitant. Unless we are of those whose existence is sometimes alleged—but has, I think never been proved—who are quite deaf to its call, we make each of us our private high-roads to where it awaits us. I know those who, when life seems a drab and savourless affair, brood on the South Seas, on coral islands and white beaches, on bread-fruit trees and happy parrakeets. Others there are (more numerous, perhaps) who turn their minds to thoughts of love—not love on its warm, comforting, domestic, companionable side, but

the strange, windy seas of passion that toss the heart like
a boat on lifting waters and sing in the soul like harps.
Some read poetry, some mystery stories, some love
stories; some think of green fields, of mountains, of
forests, or of little steep-streeted foreign towns that
smell of fish and wine; some dream of music, some of
God. This thought of God may be, for those who can
believe in God even a little, a royal road to romance.
A God at the back of, or at the heart of, this strange
business of life; some eternal, striving, courageous will,
calling to human wills for strife and courage too; this,
for those who can think it, has the wonder and the
beauty of a poem. The quest for a God who may be
apprehended and found among the queer paradoxes,
anguishes, and turmoils of the world, or in the peace
of lonely places, or in the lit and chanted poetry of
churches, or in the conflicts of the soul, or, indeed, anywhere men choose to seek him—this has been one of
the age-old romances of the human race. Round it,
and round the further and more recent thought of the
martyred Christ of the Gospel, the living Christ of
the Churches, the mystic Christ in the human soul, men
have woven splendid dreams, reared them from earth to
sky, built of them soaring palaces in stone. The Plymouth Brother in his unlovely house of prayer, the
Catholic in his tawdry church adorned with plaster
images and gilt hearts, the Anglican at Matins or at
Mass, the Unitarian in his sensible modern chapel, the
Israelite in his synagogue, the Quaker at his meeting—
before them all there runs this strange and mystic road,

losing itself in limitless horizons. For them all life should be as full of wonder and adventure as the world of the child, an enchanted *terra incognita* waiting exploration. All believers in God are not romantic; nor, for that matter, are all lovers, nor even quite all sailors. But they have the keys to romance in their hands, to use if they will.

For that matter, so have we all. This vast and curious universe, with its impenetrable destinies, these wild and spinning masses lit by strange fires, dashing hither and thither to destruction through cold and illimitable space, or running obediently round and round and round, like the squirrel in its cage, this singular planet we ourselves adorn, humming with its queer freight of animal and vegetable life, its squalor and materialism lit, as by wavering candles, by beauty, by valour, and by dreams—certainly the whole universe is built of the very fabric of romance.

But, if you are reluctant to brood over the universe, or weary of so doing (and it is, in truth, an exhausting object for contemplation), and yet desire romance, you can always go to the pictures, or to the Zoo aquarium, or for a day in the country. Or, if by ill chance you are too straitened in means for any of these, you can stand in the street and wait until a fire engine, with its wild, clanging bell, dashes by. Be sure, in any case, that romance is not far to seek.

# CHRISTMAS PRESENTS

THE happy season of Christmas is, alas! at hand once again. It must be at hand, for, though the leaves still shake yellow on the trees and the world still wears its autumnal mien, already Christmas canticles shrill about street and lane, and the shops have burgeoned once more into those silver spangles, that scarlet bunting, by which they acknowledge Yule. Once again, then, we bow to that tyranny of custom which sends us out to buy and buy, to empty our purses and expend our time and strength, to draw up lists of those who must receive from us, and of the objects we destine for them; to lay in stores of brown paper and of string, to wait in sullen queues in post offices among crowds as foolish as ourselves.

Why we make this havoc of a perfectly good fortnight out of each year is a question only to be answered by those who can also tell us why we seat ourselves round tables at regular hours and eat absurdly served meals, why we load our bodies with apparel of a monstrously inconvenient material and shape; why, in fact, we practise any of the foolish ritual of our daily life here below. For that matter, I can answer all these questions myself—we do these things because they are done.

And, since they are done, and since, unfortunately,

the time appears to have arrived to do this one of them ("Post Early," we are annually bidden, and, in response to the parrot cry, we post a little earlier each year, and shall soon be posting for Christmas in August)—since, I say, the time would seem to have arrived for making this havoc of our lives, we must either proceed to make it with a good grace, or, with an equal grace, nay, with more, for more is needed— to refuse to make it. This latter course only, after all, needs a little strength of mind, a little of that calm pride which is above being troubled by the un- spoken reproaches of relations and friends. Be sure the great philosophers have been, and are, untroubled by Christmas. Receive presents they may, but give them they will not. This is the best attitude, for such as have the necessary strength of purpose.

But you and I are not among these. You and I sit down and make lists; we slink into shops and try to buy; we have not the nerve to receive without giv- ing, nor (least of all) to neglect those great and un- giving receivers, the young. Children rightly regard themselves as infinitely entitled to receive, infinitely free from the burden of giving (once their immediate families are lightly and cheaply disposed of). They are wiser than their spendthrift elders; they, parsimonious little creatures, know the worth of each penny, and pre- cisely what value it will, if well spent, provide for them. One should, I think, always give children money, for they will spend it for themselves far more profitably than we can ever spend it for them.

Money, then, for the young. Thus, the children question happily settled, we can consider adults. There are those who say that all our presents should be bestowed on those who cannot afford to purchase what they require for themselves. There is much to be said for this view. So much, indeed, is there to be said for and against any view about giving presents, that it is safer not to think about it, but to buy your presents first, and afterwards to consider what, if anything, you will do with them. After all, if you decide in the end not to give them to anyone, you can always keep them. It is well, then, in buying presents, to bear that contingency in mind. In fact, perhaps the best question to ask yourself, as you stroll through those glittering Babylons where objects intended for Christmas gifts are stored, is not, What shall I give? but, What should I like to have?

And, once you begin asking yourself this, you are hopelessly entangled in the snares. Nearly everything you see seems infinitely desirable. Here is a family group—a St. Bernard dog with real hair, and two puppies. What a possession! Near it is a miniature table laid for breakfast, with boiled eggs, teapot, and telephone; and at the table, just about to use the telephone, sits a black bear, I should like to have that breakfast-table very much. Here, too, is a mother kangaroo, with baby kangaroo in pouch. And an infinite number of railway-trains and little motor-cars and dolls-houses; and even a model of Wembley.

Or would you rather have a punch-ball, or a boudoir-cap, or bath salts, or ping-pong, or a set of theatre-tickets? All these, I see, are to be had. All, certainly, would be engaging possessions. For that matter so would a motor-car like a flying beetle, which should spread its wings and fly when required, and then alight and run. Of such a car I have heard, but no one has seen it yet; and I shall neither give nor receive it for Christmas. More probably, I shall give and receive a little lady shaped like a pin-cushion and a little suède-bound copy of the Maxims of Marcus Aurelius or St. Francis. That is more my level and yours. But even these—or, anyhow, the pin-cushon lady—we shall like when we receive them, so great is the joy of receiving a present at all. Giving is not at all interesting; but receiving is, there is no doubt about it, delightful. I see scarcely anything in any of the shops, nor can I think of anything, which I should not like to receive, which would not noticeably brighten my life. Short of the kangaroo with young, of the breakfast-table with bear, even a little plasticine would please me. Anything which I obtained thus, at the expense of another, would be joyful. A present—there is magic in the word.

Straying thus happily in the glittering Babylons, we have forgotten the reason for which we are here. We caress each object with our eyes and hands, seeing it as a potential present, until, with a shock, we are recalled to harsh reality by—"Can I serve you with anything?"—and we remember that, until Christmas Day dawns, we are but buyers and givers, not those lords of creation, receivers.

Are there those, I wonder, of more generous mould, who are natural givers, and think in shops not, What should I like to have? but, What should I like to give? Probably. The human race is infinitely admirable. And, indeed, these others are wiser, for giving is in their own hands, while receiving must wait on destiny. . . . But I cannot believe that their joy is as great.

# SOME INQUIRIES

# INTO THE SANCTITY OF THE HOME

THE Sanctity of the Home. Around this stimu-
lating and noble phrase, what battles have been
waged, what bishops have ridden forth to tilt, what
womanly women and manly men have penned epistles
for Ealing and Acton to their favourite journals! For
four hundred years (at least) we have heard it in this
country; for as many, inquiring minds have wondered,
each time it crossed their paths, precisely what is
meant.

And this brings us to a question which has always
puzzled me, What homes have sanctity? Is a bachelor
or spinster home insusceptible of this grace, as (we
are told) women are insusceptible of the grace of Holy
Orders? Can a flat have sanctity? Can a boarding-
house? Can a hotel? How does one know whether
sanctity adorns one's home or not? And is sanctity
a gift undivided and complete (like Orders) which a
home either has or has not, or is it more like a sense
of humour, which has degrees? Can a home have a
little sanctity but not much, or is it an all-or-nothing
business? And is it there from the beginning, from the
first Michaelmas when you move in, or does it slowly
grow with residence? One imagines the former, for
the users of the phrase seem to assume that it is a fix-

ture, until it is tampered with, undermined, and destroyed.

Sometimes it is in the plural. "Woman," it has been well said, "completes her destiny by occupying herself with the industries and sanctities of the home." I am even less sure of its meaning in the plural than in the singular. Industries I know, too well: but sanctities are not the same as industries, for both are mentioned separately. Has my home sanctities? Do I occupy myself with them? Do I, in short, complete my destiny? Are they, these sanctities, concerned with the wall-papers, the pipes, the floors? If the marriage laws should be tampered with, would the sanctities, as well as the sanctity, of my home suffer? Could a home lose sanctity and yet keep some sanctities? Has the home in which I dwell either the one or the others? In my heart, alas, I suspect it of little (or few) of either.

What is to be done about it? The less to lose, you will say, when these terrible destructive laws are passed. They will not undermine my home. All the same, I scarcely like to be left out of this business. If there are sanctities going, I feel I should like to have some for my flat. How, then, are they to be obtained, that I may occupy myself with them and thereby complete my destiny?

A further question arises. Can the home of an unmarried man have sanctity or sanctities? (I do not ask does it, but can it?) I suspect not. I suspect that celibate man—and possibly celibate woman, too—is insusceptible of this grace. (I speak, of course, of

modern man, not of the holy hermits of old.) His
home may have industries, but sanctities, no. He must
complete his destiny, if at all, by some other means.
Indeed, I know not how a man completes his destiny.
A woman, I have heard, takes to herself a mate and
reproduces her kind, and is thereby complete; with a
woman completion, I believe, signifies multiplication
(when it does not signify the above-mentioned mysterious occupation with the sanctities of the home).
As to a man, I doubt if even multiplication completes
him; possibly nothing completes him; possibly he remains an imperfect creature to the end.

Why these distinctions should be I do not know;
mine not to reason why, but merely to record what I
hear said. On the face of it, one would think that
we must needs all complete our destinies, merely by
the simple process of living out our lives to the end.
But we are not to-day investigating the meaning of
the word destiny; doubtless that, too, has its strange
interpretation which might profitably be examined; at
the moment, however, we are considering Sanctity.

The more I think of Sanctity, the more desirable it
seems. Not the false and hypocritical sanctity referred
to by the anti-Puritan gentleman who wrote, in the
year 1616, of "Puritanes, by whose apparent shew Of
sanctity doe greater evils grow," but the real thing.
How delightful it must be in a home! I could wish
mine filled with sanctities, smelling sweet to heaven
like flowers. I should like to occupy myself with them
from morning until night.

But there is but one kind of sanctity which I see any chance of obtaining for my home, and small chance of that. This is sanctity in its sense of inviolability. The "inviolable refuge of the home"— what untrue words are these! In truth, nothing can be less inviolable than the home, for the reason that its locality is known, or can be readily discovered. If you desire the sanctity of inviolability, you should have no home; you should travel abroad, and nightly pitch your moving tent, leaving no address behind you. But sanctity in the home! What a dream before dawn is here, what a vision through the ivory gates!

Nevertheless, you may do something towards attaining a little of it. You may remove your telephone receiver; you may placard your door with "Out. Small-pox. Go away," or "Beware of the hyena," or "Dead of leprosy; not yet buried." You may send a notice to the *Times,* and request No Flowers. By such means you may win for your home a little temporary and precarious sanctity. But be sure it will never be much.

No; if you want that kind of sanctity, you must do without a home. You can have in your home (if you are a person of good character) the sanctity provided by your own virtue; or (if you are married) the sanctity which means a state of undivorced matrimony and nothing more.

But as to sanctities (and it is these that I really covet for my home) they are "a deep, conceal'd and precious misterie," and, for I know not what mystic reason, I suspect them of numbering seven. And possibly my home has a full tale of them, only how shall I know them? Like orgies, they are nameless; you shall not lay your hand on one of them and say, "Here is a sanctity," as who should capture and hold a flea.

Another inquiry. How many sanctities, added together, make sanctity? For that matter (and talking of insects), how many moths make moth?

And this is my last inquiry, since I anticipate satisfactory answers to none of them.

## INTO HUMAN SPEECH

WHY does no one take in hand the brightening of the census? At present it is, as planned, a deplorably tedious affair, worthy of the stale bureaucratic minds which conceived it. Given that the State permits itself to make impertinent inquiries of the individuals whom it dominates, why make such dull ones? These are the things which matter least about people —the place of their abode, their temporary occupation, the year of their birth. Why not ask something worth asking, such as "Do you believe in a God? If so, what, if any, meaning do you attach to the word God? How many love affairs have you had? Trace (outline only) the course of each. What, if anything, do you read, and why?" and so forth. But, above all, I should include in the question form a series of inquiries on the use and meanings of words. "(1) In what sense do you personally use the words (a) suggestive, (b) literally, (c) problem novel, (d) spinster, (e) decimated, (f) annihilated, (g) nominal (and so on, throughout the alphabet). Give examples. (2) State whether or not you consider that you employ these words correctly, or whether you desire to do so."

Many replies would, if truthfully given, run as follows:—

(1) Suggestive: indecent or improper. *Example:* "Too many film scenarios are suggestive."

Literally: nearly. *Example*: "My dear, I am literally dead with fatigue."

Problem novel: a serious and unpleasant story, probably about men and women. *Example*: "I want something light and nice to read, please. Not a problem novel."

Spinster: a disagreeable woman of advanced years, preferably unmarried. *Example*: "Unkind people called her a spinster, but she scarcely deserved this harsh name."

Decimated: very greatly reduced in numbers. *Example*: "The troops were literally decimated."

Annihilated: see decimated. *Example*: "The troops were literally annihilated."

Nominal: small. *Example*: "The rent is nominal."

(2) I do not know whether or not I use these words correctly. I have never thought about it, and should be incapable of arriving at any conclusions on the subject were I to do so, as I have not a clear head. I do not suffer from the desire to which you allude.

The answers should, in the interests of a greater mutual comprehension, be made public. For—it is idle to blink the fact—we are, as regards the language we use, strangers and foreigners one to the other, with echoing straits between us thrown. One is pulled up at every turn by some curiously used phrase. One opens one's morning or evening paper, and lo, some half-wit has written to tell the editor that in his opinion some cinematograph film, some picture, some book, even some fashion in ladies' attire, is "suggestive." He does not say of what. Someone else writes to protest that the said film, picture, book or garment is no such thing; it suggests nothing; it is not, to use the dictionary definition, calculated or fitted to suggest thoughts or ideas. This is understood to be praise. It is notoriously a bad thing to suggest thoughts or ideas. As Mr. Chesterton somewhere remarks, ideas are dangerous, but the man to whom they are most dangerous is the man of no ideas. So those writers to newspapers, scenting an idea far off, fly from it in truly British horror, sure that it must be a bad one. So they have actually come to use the word suggestive as synonymous with indecent. "Suggestive pictures," they say, condemning them, in the interests, possibly, of pure form and line, joining the campaign, perhaps, against the literary picture. But—a picture which should suggest nothing—no thought, no comment, no idea! What a picture!

There is, indeed, a curious tendency to degrade words, to attribute to them objectionable meanings when they have none by right. The mind of man is notoriously corrupt, and since then all he has loved to see was evil where none is. The English language is full of examples of this. "Now used in a bad sense" —this is the most frequent of dictionary comments on words. How seldom one sees, "Now used in a good sense." The movement of the words, like that of water, is downwards, not upwards. Take, for instance, "problem," as applied to the contents of a novel. "All these unhealthy problem novels," robust-minded people were fond of saying in the youth of our parents. But a problem, as such, is rather a healthy exercise for the mind than otherwise. "I don't want a problem novel," I heard a young man say at the *Times* Book Club the other day. The book offered him and accepted in reply to this was called *What Is It?* or *Who Was It?* or something of that sort. Surely this must have been a problem novel, if ever there was one. I mentioned this, after the young man had gone, to the intelligent young lady who had served him. "Oh," she said, "he meant by a problem novel something serious; one of those novels about sex, and that." And he probably did. She and he talked the same strange language and understood one another. Sex, and that. That means men and women. Well, most novels are about these. So most novels are problem novels. But what *I* mean by a problem novel is one with a mystery, a hidden criminal or treasure. Is sex a problem? Surely, in most cases, not in the least. Nothing could be simpler. "Sex," by the way, is another maligned, unjustly used word. "A sex story," people will say, meaning, in their own half-witted language, a suggestive story, a dubious story (that is another good word —dubious). But what is wrong with sex, with being a man or a woman (which so few of us can avoid) that we should confound it with impropriety? This downward drag of the human mind at harmless words is ominous. Take "spinster," for instance. I read in a newspaper the other day that April was shedding "not girlish tears, but spinsterish drops." What strange antithesis had the writer in his mind? Did he know that "spinster" is the feminine equivalent of "bachelor," and means "unmarried female who has attained marriageable age," and that its antithesis is not girl, but matron? He obviously did not know it; perhaps (even if he should happen on this article) he will never know it. And there are thousands in his case, who honestly believe in their poor fuddled minds that the word does not refer merely to matrimonial status, but to advanced years, or defects of disposition, or both.

It would be interesting to trace the psychological causes of all these misuses. The use, for instance, of "literally" where "metaphorically" is meant, as in "literally a mother to him," "literally dead," and so on, is probably due to what has been called oppositionism, i.e., the use of words in senses directly opposed to their correct meaning, in order to achieve some bizarre effect. The common misuse of "'decimated" is doubtless meiosis, i.e., under-statement to heighten effect, like "not half." The misuse of "annihilated" seems to arise from a desire for over-statement. The curious use of "object," in such phrases as "distance, or expense, no object," is doubtless a survival of an old use of object (obsolete in all phrases but this) as meaning hindrance or obstacle. This is a rather interesting example of the habit of phrases, mentioned by Mr. Pearsall Smith, of surviving exclusively among illiterate people.

And then, apart from single words, what strange uses of phrase are there! What superfluous repetitions of the already stated. "Well, I said, I'm not going to stay here any more, I said, if that's the way I'm treated, I said." Is the speaker afraid that the hearer may get confused as to which person in his story was speaking, so that he feels impelled to make it quite clear? One would value a first-hand reason for these "I saids." Then there is the curious locution "if you know what I mean," a conditional clause which yet appears to depend on nothing. "One feels one can always trust him to do the decent thing, if you know what I mean." Does this mean that the speaker's trust in his friend depends on his hearer knowing what he means, or is it the decent conduct of his friend which depends on this knowledge? The sentence, susceptible of either interpretation, doubtless bears neither. But no one has ever explained what it does mean. And it is no use asking, for no one will tell you. The poverty of the answers we most of us give to such inquiries is only equalled by the strangeness of our questions. "Where's your light?" some one will call out to a passing bicyclist. What answer does the questioner expect to such a question? Where, indeed, are lights as yet unkindled? I suppose the correct answer would be "No light of mine occupies at this moment any point in space." My light. The light that would be burning in my lamp were I to kindle it there. What a question to be asked, and by no student of philosophy, but by a half-educated youth in a village street. Half-educated. Most curious and inaccurate phrase of all. Take education, in its ideal fullness, which has never been attained on this planet nor ever will be, and bisect it. The fraction thus obtained far exceeds the desire or deserts of any human being. To be half-educated would be indeed a great and glorious state. The half-educated would know the meanings of the words they used (unless, indeed, that branch of knowledge happened to be included in the half which was lacking to them). "Uneducated" is a more inaccurate word still, since not even the meanest of us is quite that. "Only very slightly educated" is what we really mean. It is also what we really are; and if we go on as we are there will not, in a hundred years' time, be a single word remaining to us which we all use in the same sense.

## INTO EVENING PARTIES

HUMAN beings are curious creatures, and in nothing more curious than in the forms of diversion which they devise for themselves. Some of these are quite comprehensible; they give physical or mental pleasure. Bathing in the sea, for instance; or watching a play; or visiting the Zoo; or eating agreeable food at someone else's expense, or even at one's own; or playing some game with a ball. It is easy to understand that having one's person surrounded by water, in which one floats and swims, or watching human life enacted improbably by others on a stage, or seeing strange beasts in cages, or rolling elegant foods about the palate, or chasing after a ball, is pleasing. But, besides these simple pleasures, humanity has devised some so-called amusements which seem to depend for their reputations as entertainments less on pleasing sensations inflicted on the participants than on some convention which has ordained that these pursuits shall be held agreeable. It speaks well, perhaps, for the kindliness and amiability of the human race that most such pursuits are of a gregarious nature. Assembling together; dearly we love to do this. "Neglect not the assembling of yourselves together," says (I think) St. Paul somewhere; and it was a superfluous piece of admonition. Neglect of this will never be numbered among the many omissions of mankind. Seeing one another; meeting the others of our race; exchanging remarks; or merely observing in what particular garments they have elected to clothe themselves to-day; this is so nearly universal a custom that it has become dignified into an entertainment, and we issue to one another invitations to attend such gatherings.

We issue them and we accept them, and, when the appointed date arrives, we assume such of our clothes as we believe to be suitable to the gathering, and sally forth to the party of pleasure. Often, indeed usually, it is in the evening. Therefore we clothe ourselves in such garb as men and women have agreed, in their strange symbolism, to consider appropriate to the hours after eight o'clock or so. And perhaps—who knows?—it is in the exercise of this savage and primitive conventionalism that a large part of the pleasure of an evening gathering consists. We are very primitive creatures, and the mere satisfaction of self-adornment, and of assuming for a particular occasion a particular set of clothes, may well tickle our sensibilities. Be that as it may, we arrive at our party dolled, so to speak, up, and find ourselves in a crowd of our fellow-creatures, all dolled up too. Now we are off. The party of pleasure has begun. We see friends and talk to them. But this we could do with greater comfort at our own homes or in theirs; this cannot, surely, be the promised pleasure. As a matter of fact, if you succeed in getting into a corner with a friend and

talking, be sure you will be very soon torn asunder by
an energetic hostess, whose motto is "Keep them moving." We are introduced to new acquaintances. This
may, no doubt, be very agreeable. They may be persons you are glad to know. But it is doubtful whether
your acquaintanceship will prosper very much to-night.
It may well be that no topics suitable for discussion
will present themselves to either of you at the moment
of introduction. I know someone who says that she
never can think of anything to say to persons introduced to her at a party except "Do you like parties?"
And that is too crude; it simply cannot be said. You
must think of some more sophisticated remark. Having thought of it, you must launch it, in the peculiarly
resonant pitch necessary to carry it above the clamour
(for this clamour, which somewhat resembles the
shrieking of a jazz band, is an essential accompaniment
to a party, and part of the entertainment provided). A
conversation will then ensue, and must be carried on
until one or other of you either flags or breaks away,
or until someone intervenes between you. One way
and another, a very great deal gets said at a party. Let
us hope that this is a good thing. It is apparent, anyhow, that the mere use of the tongue, quite apart from
the words it utters, gives pleasure to many. If it gives
you no pleasure, and if, further, you derive none from
listening to the remarks of others, there is no need to
converse. You had better then take up a position in a
solitary corner (if possible on a chair, but this is a rare
treat) and merely listen to the noise as to a concert,

not endeavouring to form out of it sentences. As a matter of fact, if thus listened to, the noise of a party will be found a very interesting noise, containing a great variety of different sounds. If you are of those who like also to look at the clothes of others, you will, from this point of vantage, have a good view of these.

It is very possible, however, that you have only come to the party on the chance of obtaining something good to eat. This is, after all, as good a reason as another. You will, with any luck, be offered some comestible—a sandwich, or a chocolate, or some kind of a drink, or, if you are very fortunate, an ice. With a view to this, you cannot do better than to stand solitary, so that your host or hostess may, in despair of making you talk, give you to eat. If you have eaten or drunk, you have anyhow got something out of the party; you can say, in recalling it, "I ate two chocolates, and that sandwich pleased me," or, better still, "I drank." Words spoken are empty air, and drift windily into oblivion; and, anyhow, there are greatly too many of these; but about food and drink there is something solid and consoling. An hour in which you have consumed nourishment is seldom an hour spent in vain.

But far be it from me to suggest that we should, or do, take such pains over attiring ourselves, and go to so much trouble, and possibly expense, in travelling from one house to another, merely for the sake of some foolish edible trifle which could be procured and consumed with greater ease in the home. I am convinced that the majority of human creatures do not go to parties for the sake of any food, or even drink, that they may get there. No; the reason (if reason indeed there is beyond blind habit) is, fundamentally, that primitive instinct to take any chance of herding together which led our earliest forefathers to form tribes, village communities, and cities. It is the same reason for which great spaces of the countryside in all lands stand empty, while those who might live there herd, instead, in hideous, shrieking and dreadful cities. It is, in short, the gregarious instinct, based on fear of solitude, on terror of such dangers and uncanny visitants as may, we feel, attack us unless we hide within the crowd. We are a haunted race, fleeing from silence and great spaces, feeling safe only when surrounded by warm, comprehensible, chattering humanity like ourselves. So, when there comes for us a little pasteboard card inscribed with an address where, and a date when, we may thus surround ourselves, under some hospitable roof, we may say with our minds and lips, "Shall I go to this!" casually, as if it mattered not at all; but deep down in our hidden souls the primal whisper sounds—"There will be people there. There is safety in a crowd. Go!"

This is, at least, what I presume occurs in that buried self of which we know so little. Anyhow, for one reason or another, go we do, quite often. And if anyone knows of any other reason why, I should be glad to hear it.

Not that, personally, I do not enjoy parties. . . .

## INTO QUESTIONS AND ANSWERS

THE impulse to ask questions is among the more primitive human lusts. You will meet it in the infant, which, directly it can utter, will propound its imbecile queries. "What is that?" it will ask, and "Why?" and "What would happen if . . . ?" Infants are, in this respect as in so many others, insufficiently thwarted. They are allowed to grow up still asking questions. Indeed, they hear their elders doing so all day long. Questions to which the answer can be of no conceivable importance to the inquirer are bandied about as part of the normal human interchange of amenities. "How do you do?" people ask, and stay not for an answer. "How are you?" they inquire, and would not for the world be told. No wonder that the child continues on his questioning way. Everyone asks him impertinent questions, and how should he not retaliate? His personal habits are inquired into by relatives: "Have you washed your hands? Your ears? Your neck? Have you been good to-day?" His age, his plans for his future life, are asked after by acquaintances, who do not in the least want information about either. Even his religion is presented to him in the guise of inquiry. "What is your name? Who gave you this name? What else did they give you?

What is your duty?" What, why, when, who, how, why not otherwise. . . . Bored and exasperated with answering such foolish conundrums, the infant resolves that he will at least be revenged. He will not only an answerer but a questioner be. And so he is, and so he remains through life.

His life, as the lives of others, is full of vain and tedious questionings. "Where have you been? Whom did you meet? What did they say? Are you back already?" The best answer is another question. "Why do you want to know?" I was told the other day of a young man who was out walking with an older man when they met an acquaintance of the latter's, who inquired genially, "Is that your son?" The youth was somewhat surprised to hear his companion immediately and unhesitatingly answer, "Yes." Supposing that his elderly friend had his reasons, he let it pass, but inquired afterwards, "What made you tell him that?" to which the simple and quite adequate reply was, "What the devil business was it of his?" What, indeed? One might do worse than always use this formula in reply to unnecessary inquisition. No, not always. There are questioners who must be answered according to their folly. Of such are officials of Passport Offices, with their parrot-like cries of "Where were you born? When? Why? Where were your parents born? What colour is your hair? Does it curl? Are you deformed? Are you a polygamist? Why do you want to go abroad?" Impertinent and offensive as such inquiries must be to the sensitive and well-bred mind, they must be answered, if you really, on further consideration, do want to go abroad. They need not be answered correctly, but some sort of a story about yourself, your hair, your parents, and your reasons, if any, for existing, must be put together. "What the devil business is it of yours?" might be an answer satisfactory to yourself, but be sure it will get you no further from your native shores.

On the other hand, I commend it to members of His Majesty's government in parliament assembled, what time they are teased by the foolish inquisitiveness on this and that of members, without which the House of Commons is unable to begin its daily business. Is His Majesty's Government aware that there is trouble in China, traffic in the streets, and so on and so forth? What, if anything, do His Majesty's Government intend to do about it? Do not, gentlemen, I entreat you, reply to these inquiries in the painstaking manner to which you are used, having disturbed the civil service officials to instruct you what to say. Return a sharp counter inquiry such as I suggest, and you will both snub the inquisitiveness of questioners and relieve the tedium of question time.

For unofficial inquirers also this form of reply, or the more temperate "Do you indeed wish to know, and if so why?" might well serve. One might have both forms printed on postcards, and send one or another, according to mood, in reply to those letters which one receives occasionally from periodicals, asking "Are married people happier than single?" "Is poetry a necessity to man?" "How many hours do you work a day?" (the impertinence of it!) "Should women be educated?" (There seem to be, for some reason, more inquiries raised about women than about most other topics.) "Do you approve of divorce?" "What sort of pen do you prefer?" Personally I reply, truly, to most such inquiries that I cannot understand the question. In point of fact, there are very few questions so worded that I do quite understand them. Other people seem to do so. Long replies are elicited, I do not say *to* the questions, but round them. Nearly everyone seems to know whether married persons or single are the happier, what "poetry" means, and what "necessity," whether women should be educated, and how many hours, if any, they work a day. But for those like myself, who seldom, if ever, know these things, or even understand what is the question at issue, there should be some recognised counter-offensive such as I suggest. Why, sir or madam, do you want to know? Why the devil, for that matter, does anyone ever want to know anything? One supposes it is because life is itself an eternal and eternally unanswered question, and so spawns an infinitesimal number of smaller questions as it stumbles along its puzzled way. The Eastern question, the Housing question, the Honours question, the Woman question, the Man question. . . . Is there a God? Should maniacs marry? Why look old sooner than you need? Such inquiries, and a myriad more, are fired in an unceasing barrage by bewildered man as he proceeds, defending himself thus against the tremendous riddle of the universe, which must otherwise stun him with its onslaught.

So let us by all means ask questions one of another, and endeavour to persuade ourselves that the answers matter. "Are we to have it fine?" we ask. "How is your wife? Have you seen the news? Do you know Smith? Have you read anything lately? Seen any plays? Been abroad? What's to happen in the East? Are we to have longer skirts—crinolines—an election— a war? Did you see the aeroplane writing Zambuk on the sky?"

There are various defences against the attack. You may use such a counter-inquiry as I have suggested above (but that is rude). You may lie (but that is wrong). You may gape like a half-wit and say you do not know (but that causes you to be despised). You may say, "Ah, that's telling!" (but that is arch) you may say, politely but coldly, "Unless you really want to know very badly, I think I would rather not say, as I have not much time just now" (but that is priggish). Or you may yield, put up your hands defeated, and reply with the truth so far as you know it (but that is weak).

The best method is to retort with a fusillade of questions of your own, so rapid and unintermittent that your adversary is bewildered. Thus, to "Been away lately? What's to happen in the East?" you may reply sharply, "Been sick lately? What's to happen in the West? Many mice in your house? How many cigarettes do you smoke a day? When did you last get your hair cut? Why did you marry your husband (or wife)? Do you grow calceolarias? Ever been in gaol? What do you think of the Bolivian banking system?" and so on and so forth, without pause for reply, until your companion has disappeared. The game is then to you, and the probabilities are that next time that particular inquirer wants to know anything, he will ask someone else.

You can also try this form of reply should you be so unfortunate as to be asked one of those questions which are, I believe, intended to insult, such as "Who do you think *you* are, anyway?" I have heard speculations as to the proper reply if any, to this inquiry, some being only able to think of the surely rather flat and uninspired, "As good as you, any day," others being in favour of the more sinister and alarming "Hush! I'm the emperor of China," others again of the perhaps rather crude and irrelevant "All right nasty-fyce." Personally I believe that a return fusillade of inquiries on a wide and varied range of topics would meet the case most effectively. Once acquire a reputation for this ready barrage, and you will be as nearly safe from questions as anyone may be in this inquiring world.

## INTO THINKING ALIKE UPON RELIGION

I HAVE observed, whenever the subject of a closer union between the various Christian Churches has turned up (as from time to time during the last four hundred years or so it has), a tendency on the part of some persons interested in the subject, though by no means all, to maintain that a greater degree of religious uniformity than the world at present enjoys would be an agreeable thing. This idea seems to obtain among the members of several prominent Churches. I noticed, for instance, that a Roman Catholic society recently held a meeting in the Coliseum; one of the objects of this society seemed to be that other British persons should become Roman Catholics too. And from time to time there is a clamour made by certain Protestants, whose object seems to be that other British persons should be Protestants also. You will meet religious propagandists of all shades of opinion, from Positivist to Plymouth Brother. It has always been so. The earliest Christians wanted others too to be Christians; their contemporaries, the pagans, were firmly resolved that their fellow-creatures should *not* be Christians, or, if Christians they insisted on being, that they should be so at the price of providing a Roman holiday for the public.

A curious human tendency indeed, and hard for those who do not share it to understand. For, to observers of human nature, one of the most interesting things about that very interesting business, religion, is its infinite variety of expression. To turn a Quaker into a Catholic, a Catholic into a Protestant, a Theosophist into a Wesleyan, a Plymouth Brother into a Higher Thinker—what dull, perverted aims are these! To stamp out and flatten all those interesting diversities of temperament which lead men to follow their Gods by different paths (or rather, to address them in different manners, for following is not, as a rule, what we do)—this would be a stupid enterprise indeed, but one, fortunately, impossible of achievement. For never shall one of nature's anti-ritualists be happy in ceremonious worship, or a born Catholic religious without sacraments and creeds, or a Protestant anything but sceptical of Church authority and papal infallibility, or a cultured cathedral Anglican anything but offended by the hymns and prayers alike of Catholics, Protestants and Ethicists. We cannot get away from the fact that it helps some worshippers to sing hymns by Faber and Messrs. Moody and Sankey, while others cannot so much as read them without a shudder of distaste. These tastes and distastes are facts in human nature, which cannot be roughly ridden over. While, as to creeds, you will never do away with the facts that some like the Apostles' and the Nicene, some can recite, with intelligence and agreement, that of Athanasius (which revolts others), and that the creed of one religious sect contains (I am told) the cryptic clause, "I believe in hawthorn when it is white." It seems unlikely that all these persons should ever be happy reciting the same creed and singing the same hymns in the same kind of church. And why should they attempt to be so? What would be gained by such *rapprochements* of sundered temperaments and tastes? Many people, of course, do not mean, when they talk of union, any such uniformity, but merely inter-communion between the various branches of the Christian Church, and this certainly seems a Christian and charitable notion. But others go further, and really do seem to desire that all men should, in a sense, worship and believe alike. The Roman Catholic society referred to above says that this is its desire. Roman Catholics would say, possibly, that there is such a thing as the true religion, and that theirs is it, and that all men ought to possess truth. But for most of us there is no such thing as the true religion. There are only the varieties of religious experience, as manifested by each person.

Be that as it may, the representatives of religious bodies have always (or, anyhow, since the Age of Tolerance began) had a happy and kindly habit of meeting together in congresses, with a view, they think, to *rapprochement,* but in reality they are but fulfilling one of the fundamental impulses in human nature, such as the impulse to love, to eat, to talk, to shun death, and to meet together in congress. Meeting together to talk, from the beginning of the history of life on this planet (and it has been by no means confined to human life),

has always been a favourite amusement. Very naturally, then, since so many of us desire to do this thing,
we make all kinds of pretexts for doing it. And a
very common pretext is that to meet together and explain each to one another our several points of view on
any given topic may possibly, though improbably, assist
in the common stock of knowledge on that topic. To
the magic of the spoken word is attributed an efficacy
unattained by print, and what is called the give and
take of discussion is supposed to clarify the minds of
speakers and hearers—a theory which neither the experience of centuries nor the procession of conferences
which followed on the recent European war has destroyed.

So the religious world has its summer schools, its
congresses, its conferences, its discussions, from spring
until autumn. It is apt to have "Copec" in April,
Anglo-Catholics in July, Anglican Fellows also in July,
Pan-Protestants (if thus I name them rightly) at
Mürren in August, Modern Churchmen at Oxford the
same month. The Church Congress meets a little more
autumnally, but it is improbable that the weather is
worse.

What, then, are they all about, these gatherings?
Their aims are manifold and high—the spread of
Christianity, of peace on earth, of union among religious bodies, of Catholicism, of intelligence and the
scientific temper in churches, and so forth. Some of
these aims are (possibly) incompatible, but all are good.
And, probably, all are furthered by those gatherings

which aim at them. It is said (and it speaks well for human nature that it is so) that those who meet in congresses always part liking and understanding one another better than before they met. So an increase in mutual human esteem is, anyhow, attained. This is natural enough, since people are mostly very likable. It is pleasant to think, at Mürren, of Sir Henry Lunn, the Archbishop of Upsala, the Bishop of the Reformed Church of Hungary, Father Waggett, Dr. Glover, M. Paul Sabatier, a Methodist Bishop from America, Canon Lacey, Dr. Carnegie Simpson, and all sorts of distinguished Reformed foreigners, thus increasing mutual esteem. Pleasant, too, to think of Modern Churchmen, psychologists, philosophers and men of science, so successfully engaged at Oxford in bridging that gulf (which some perceive and others deny) between religion and science. All the same, the Modern Churchmen's conference is not apt to be quite, perhaps, so satisfactory as the Mürren conference; for really good results in the way of increase of fellowship and comprehension, they need a few Anglo-Catholics, since sympathies between Modern Churchmen and Anglo-Catholics seem a little imperfect, and a conference should always begin with a little aversion, in order that its end should shine by contrast.

But the Church Congress meets always, with such an abundance of mutual liking and respect that no increase seems possible. Every Congresser sympathises with every other, and no one seems to regret anything but that he cannot be present at every simultaneous

paper. This is an ideal state of things, and justifies all
the trouble taken.

As to results . . . Well, the results of almost any
conference may be summed up in the words of a newspaper reporter of the Mürren conference. "As to the
results of the conference, none can make answer. But
at any rate all who were present must have gained
much from an understanding of other points of view
held by men every whit as sincere as ourselves." Another good result is a fresh assertion of the fact, mentioned by Canon Barnes, that "Religion is indestructi-
ble." Indeed, it certainly must be.

But for some of us, who take pleasure in what we
read, some of the pleasantest results of these gatherings
are to be found in the correspondence pages of the
Church papers after they are over. Speaking personally, my life has recently been brightened by two
sentences culled from this correspondence. One is "We
have known long since that Protestants and Modernists
have no sense of humour"; the other is, "Every ape is
inevitably innocent."

Meanwhile, and apart from congresses, what an interesting problem it is, this adjustment of each spirit to
whatever degree of religious vision, to whatever form
of religious expression, it is capable of attaining or
using. An interesting problem, and an enthralling
spectacle for the observer of the human pageant. All
kinds of speculations arise, as to how much of his particular form of religion or no-religion each man owes
to temperament, environment, chance, or early training.

As to this last, the early instruction of many Christian parents and teachers is responsible for much of the atheism among adults; many a religious home, many a Sunday-school, is a factory of unbelief. Parents and teachers would be better advised to profess belief in nothing but the hawthorn when it is white, if that, and so create, through the healthy natural process of reaction against the last generation, dogmatic Christians. Anyhow, and be that as it may, all the varieties of religious thought, however caused, are interesting. Jews worshipping Jehovah in synagogues on Saturdays, Presbyterians refusing to play or work on Sundays, Christian Scientists, with their belief in the Great Divine Ignorance, Ethicists thinking highly, Evangelicals saved by faith, Catholics believing that they have the truth, Quakers listening silently for the voice of God, Plymouth Brethren refusing mince-pies at Christmas— what a moving pageant of the human spirit is here! Let us, by all means, unite all these bodies of people in whatever bonds charity and good sense may demand, but let us take heed that such bonds shall not, even slightly, cramp their style.

# INTO THE RIGHT TIME FOR GOOD
## RESOLUTIONS

FAR be it from me to decry good resolutions, those so necessary paving-stones of our ways. Those who attempt to do without them—to live, so to speak, from hand to mouth, episodically, without previous plan or intention—may live no worse than the resolvers, but they live like the lower animals, having abandoned the great human prerogative of willing good and choosing evil. No; all I protest against in this business of resolutions is the time we choose for making them. It will have been observed by any student of others or of himself that the principal day selected by mankind for this manufacture is the last day of each year. Resolutions are then made, hot and new, to be served up ready for use and for destruction on the first day of the next, even as hot cross buns are made on Maundy Thursday ready for demolishment on Good Friday.

Let us consider some of the many reasons why this habit, so widespread, is a bad one—as bad as nearly all habits. Consider, for one thing, the weather. Are these cold, dark, and dreary days, these long and chill nights, these bitter gusts of iced wind, these driving blizzards of snow or sleet, these cheerless, inadequate firesides, really the right setting for the new life? Does not the firmest resolution wilt in these grim dawns? Have you resolved, in some misguided moment, to rise earlier from your bed? And is this, indeed, likely to occur in an English January? Have you decided on more outdoor exercise? On a better temper? On a Continental breakfast? On a colder morning bath? On the accomplishment of more work? And are any of these likely to occur to you? You may reply that, on the other hand, you have resolved on more sleep, less exposure to the elements, a greater frankness in speaking your mind to others, more bacon for breakfast, more repose, and a hotter morning bath, and that all these resolutions stand every chance, in wintry weather, of fulfilment. But I am considering now not the connoisseur in resolutions, but the normal human being, and I believe that the resolutions less likely to be kept are those more likely to be made—the high that proved too high, the heroic for earth too hard. Transfer such resolutions to a warm summer's day (should one such, by good fortune, occur), and see how far more easily and for how far longer a period they are kept.

So much for the weather. Partly, but not wholly, allied to it, is the question of mood. We are, in the days following the Christmas energies and festivities, in a low, diminished state. The last small days of the year ebb out, and with them our spirit ebbs too. We suffer from reaction. Vanity of vanities, we feel; all is vanity—Christmas, and the so recurrent passing of the years, and the little life of man. What is man (we feel), the small, ephemeral being, that he should be making proud resolutions, grandly preparing to lead that better life which he will, assuredly, never lead? Rather let him ebb and dwindle to his appointed end, unready and unresolved; it matters not at all. Is this a mood for fine and stirring resolutions? Whereas, on the other hand, if we wait for the happy spring, when the blood races quickly and delightedly through the veins, and the wheels of being, slow no longer, revolve and spin apace, and the sap of life runs through all nature, and the merry birds and winds sing in the young green woods, and we are full of that Kruschen feeling —then is the time for resolutions. Resolve *then,* if you please, to keep fit by running so many miles a day, and you will find it easy and delightful. Resolve to rise earlier, and you will spring from your bed with a tune. Resolve on a kinder temper, and you will find that the words of your mouth are sweeter than honey; on a chillier bath, and the cold water will splash about you, a life-giving tonic; on more work, and inspired energy from the young and shining world will pour into your system; on a greater economy, and you will, surrounded by the joys that money cannot buy, be able to dispense with the wares of shops. Under the soothing charm of the May sun, persons have even been known to end, with comparative ease, such relationships as they thought should cease, and to be kind to those whom they little liked; whereas in the January bleakness one must cling to such love as warms the otherwise unwarmed world, and keep out of the way of irritants ill-borne in the cold. Let us then, in the name of common sense, defer our resolutions until the cycle of the year, of which man also is a part, shall make the new life apprehensible and natural, and let us cease the morbid and contra-natural practice of making high endeavours on a low gear.

But I have not yet mentioned the worst count against this vice. There was once a Roman Catholic, strict in his observance of Church rules, who, dining with free-thinking friends on a Friday, discovered, too late, that he had swallowed a piece of meat in his soup. "Regrettable," he remarked, "but the damage is now done"— and he proceeded with a clear conscience to consume a meat dinner; whereas, had the soup been innocuous, he would have eaten only the non-carnal portions of the meal set before him. That Friday fast was, he felt, a wash-out; no abstinence from the rest of the dinner could undo the damage done by the soup, so that he might as well make the best of it, and did so. So with the year. On January 2nd (at latest) there is over the world a great sound of rending, a mighty crack and crash. That is resolution breaking 'neath thy hand, oh man! And with that breakage goes a whole year of grace. The damage is now done; what remains but to make the best, or the worst, of it, and defer the new life for another year? Which is what we do. Whereas, were we to make our resolutions unobtrusively on some unimportant but fine summer's day, and should we by some ill chance have the misfortune to break them the day after, we should not feel that anything irretrievable had happened. We should but gather up the fragments and piece them together against the day after that. But who has the courage to gather up broken resolutions on January 2nd and mend them up for the 3rd? That year is spoilt. And thus are all the years, one after another, spoilt, and this is partly why the world and human life are as we see them.

Therefore, in the interests of morality, common sense, and the good life, I protest against this New Year's resolution habit. But my protest, alas! comes too late. The damage, I fear, is now done, and this new year has already gone to join the chronicle of wasted time.

SOME OTHER PROBLEMS OF LIFE

# A PRELIMINARY WORD

A CAREER, of one sort or another, we all must
have. It need not be an arduous career; in some
few cases it need not, even, be a financially profitable
career: but a career it must be, even if it is only the
career of the idle man or woman about town or country.

We are faced, then, in youth, with the choice of a
career. How shall we elect to spend the brief span of
our days on the upper surface of this planet? How
carefully ought young men and women to consider this
weighty question!

Women have one great advantage over men. It is
commonly thought that if they marry they have done
enough, and need career no further. If a man marries,
on the other hand, public opinion is all against him if he
takes this view. He is supposed to career all the more
strenuously for being a husband and father. The same
opinion condemns a wife and mother for careering outside her home; novels are written against her, and the
London County Council and various educational authorities shut their doors on her. So that, when a
woman marries, she has virtually made her choice of
careers. Even if she keeps servants to do the house-
work and mind any children there may be, still she has
her career.

But women who do not marry must do something

else. If they are very much disinclined or inapt for personal exertion, and very fortunately situated, they can perhaps prevail on a parent or parents to maintain them in idleness in the parent's home. Their career is then that of a parasitic loafer, or daughter-at-home. If they choose this career, they should endeavour to make themselves as agreeable as may be to their maintainers, or they may lose their position. They should affect to tolerate their parents' follies and reactionary obscurantisms, and refrain from mocking the bread of their support. They may even, with advantage, render little services, such as informing their mother what is in the newspapers, or their father what the village is saying about this or that. Having performed a few such filial acts, they may then have the rest of the day for their own amusement, and can play games, walk, talk, write poetry, drama, or unsaleable novels to their hearts' content. This career may be called the primrose path.

But to most young females it is a path not open. Most young females have to support themselves, if they can get no unrelated male creature to support them. They have to go into the houses of others and clean them for pay, or mind their young children, or cook food, or hand it, when cooked, to the consumers, or assist in selling something in a shop or making something in a factory or take down letters from dictation in an office, or teach the young, or write something that someone will pay them for writing, or study medicine or law, or stand for Parliament, or act on a stage, or nurse the sick, or go into a convent, or what not.

It is possible to support life in all these several manners. All are rather dull, but then work is a dull thing; you cannot get away from that. The only agreeable existence is one of idleness, and that is not, unfortunately, always compatible with continuing to exist at all. So work we must; the only question is, what at?

People will, no doubt, differ as to the various merits and demerits of the careers available. Personally I regard teaching the young and nursing the sick as the two hardest and most disagreeble. Sick persons and young children demand altogether too much output of exertion and trouble. They are, I imagine, the two noblest careers in the world. Few are their halfpence (and those of teachers, anyhow, will probably be fewer still, now that a conservative government is firmly in the saddle, for conservatives, very wisely, mistrust education) and many their kicks. Someone (I have always felt) must teach, someone must nurse, but let it be others, not I. Both these professions are among the very few in which it seriously matters whether they are carried on well or ill, so my advice to young men and women is, avoid them. You will be better suited by something easier and less important.

But, whatever path you may choose, you may be sure it will have its problems and its troubles. Here, set down for your guidance, are a few.

# PROBLEMS OF A JOURNALIST'S LIFE

YOUR first problem as a journalist is to decide what kind of journalist you are going to be. There are newspaper owners, editors, political journalists, leader writers, middle writers, reporters, book reviewers, dramatic critics, art critics, serial story writers, foreign correspondents, special correspondents, fashion recorders, personal gossips, Woman's Page writers, and those who write letters to the papers. The last class is the largest, and the easiest to get into. Probably you are fit to be no other kind of journalist, and this may well be your only way of ever seeing yourself in print. As the largest class of journalists, it shall be dealt with first. It may be divided roughly into two (unequal) sections—those who write letters to the press and sign them with a name (such as Sydenham, Montague of Beaulieu, Birkenhead, or L. E. Chubb) and those who write letters to the press and sign them with some noun or adjective other than a name (such as Patriot, Free Trader, or Mother of Many). It may further be divided into those who write admiring letters, beginning "Sir, As always, you have taken the only right line on this question," those who write disagreeable letters, beginning "Sir, Since the disgraceful article in your last issue, my wife, myself, and fifteen others have all given up your paper," and those who broach some other topic than the rightness or wrongness of the editor, and begin "Sir, My small dog has recently take to whistling between his teeth. I wonder if any of your readers have had a similar experience with their pets," or "Sir, It is well known that women have no sense of honour or of humour; their cradles are empty and their skirts and hair too short." Into this section come also the small group of sensible and well-informed letters which get put on central pages of the *Times*. These are always signed, and usually with the name of some peer. They are fond of Summer Time.

Writing letters to the press is a great and arduous profession, and may well take your whole time and all your stamps. You can only expect to get a small proportion of them printed, however many you write. You will find it advisable to write to different papers with different pseudonyms. For the *Times,* "Sydenham" is not a bad one. For the *New Statesman,* something sensible and Fabian (avoid J. R. Macdonald). For the *Nation* something Liberal, with perhaps a Manchester address. Not till you get down to the penny press should you, as a rule, adopt adjectives or common nouns—though you may risk "Anti-Bolshevik" or "Patriot" in the *Morning Post.* For the *Church Times,* "Anglo-Catholic" or "Sacerdotus" goes. As to the contents of your letter, the *Spectator* will like to hear about your dog or cat, the *Nation* about some bird you may have noticed out of doors (you had better, with intelligent papers, keep to topics such as these, not try to refer to politics or economics, which will be above your capacity). You can tell the *Morning Post* anything favourable about the Dominions or Ulster which you have observed, or anything unfavourable about Bolshevists, Liberals, or the Irish Free State; you can complain to any paper about income-tax forms, to the *Daily Mail* about foreigners, to the *Westminster Gazette* about tariff duties, and to the *Church Times* about Dr. Barnes. When in despair about getting any of them printed anywhere, begin, "Sir, How right you always are!"

Enough about this (after all) inferior section of the fraternity of journalists. I have expatiated on it at too great length, its bulk must be my excuse. Let us pass to newspaper owners. The great problem for a newspaper owner is to produce a newspaper which will sell so greatly as to pay its expenses. This is very seldom done—only by a few dailies and a few of the brighter and chattier other periodicals. Most of the more intelligent press has to be subsidised. Of course this is a very good plan, if you are fortunate enough to find anyone at once so foolish and so wealthy as to subsidise your journal. If you are not, there are three courses to adopt—either a paper pays its way and goes on, or does not pay its way and does not go on, or does not pay its way but goes on just the same. Your paper will probably adopt the second of these courses, which is the most usual with papers. But, while it yet continues, you may find it quite good fun. You can put into it all the things you have always wished were in other papers. You can see that the editor writes the kind of articles you wish to have written, instead of the foolish and tedious stuff written by other editors. You can sack the whole staff at any moment (if you have been careful as to the contracts you allowed them to make). You can live in one of the Home Counties and enjoy the pleasures of a country life. You are immeasurably above journalists, for you can order journalists about, causing their pens to run with venom or honey at your pleasure. Further, you need know nothing yourself; you can leave the sordid acquisition of facts to your staff; all you have to say is, Take this line, or Take that. It is a princely life—while it lasts. Enjoy it while you may.

Let me descend to those who write in papers themselves. Even editors have to do this. They have to write articles on the Situation. Usually the situation is not of the slightest importance, but writers on it have to pretend that it is. Sometimes it is political, sometimes international, sometimes nothing in particular. Whatever it is, editors must comment on it (*a*) in such a way as to make it sound important, (*b*) from the point of view that they and their readers are accustomed to take. Casual and frivolous comments are no use, and will only depreciate the credit of your paper. If, for instance, your owner does not care for some politician, you must say so, gravely and firmly. If there is a political election, you must take a side. Editors, even if Gallios at heart, must not show it. After a general election, you must say, if your side has been defeated, "The temporary wave of madness which has passed over us in no way represents the true feeling of the

country, but is due to a number of subsidiary causes."
If your side has been successful, all you need say is
"Once again the people of Britain have spoken, with
their usual decision and calm good sense." Whatever
you do, you must have it that the people of Britain are
*on your side*. It does not do to seem to disagree with
this great people, even when they are possessed by a
temporary evil influence. You must never, on any account, say "The people of Britain are wrong, as usual,
the damned idiots. They never had any sense and probably never will have." For you must recollect that it is
the people of Britain (or some of them) who read your
paper. Sections, on the other hand, of the people of
Britain, such as Conservatives, Liberals, Socialists, and
so forth, you may allude to with distaste, for these, however numerous, do not represent the Great Mind of the
Nation. Above all, a political editor must remember
that his party and his party leaders are invariably right,
however oddly they appear to be behaving. As to the
leaders of the other parties, it is as well to get Lord Birkenhead, or Mr. E. T. Raymond, or Mr. Philip Gue-
dalla, to do a series of articles on them. This will soon
show them up in their proper colours.

Not all the editors are political. You may be a literary editor, and edit either (*a*) a whole literary paper,
such as the *London Mercury,* or *John o' London's
Weekly,* or (*b*) the literary part of an ordinary paper.
Both are sad lives. The chief trouble of (*a*) is the
articles and stories and poems which people send you,
and some of which (unless you write the whole paper

yourself, which is economical but takes time) you will have to put in and pay for, and they are not worth it, for they look very silly on the page. The chief trouble of (*b*) is the books which publishers send you, and which you have to get reviewed, and these are not worth it either. With reviewing itself we will deal presently, under *Criticism*.

You may be, on the other hand, and more probably, not an editor at all. Even so, you may still have to write leading articles, for you may be kept as a leader writer. If yours is a morning paper, you may be required any night to sit down and write suitable comments on one or another of the day's events. The chief thing to remember when you do this is that you must try not to be too greatly out of accord with the sentiment usually expressed in your paper. Only the editor (or more usually, the owner) may perform a volte-face; it is not for such as you; in fact, your leader will not be printed if you do. You should not aim, in leaders, at originality, epigram, or smartness; you will probably not achieve these things, and you might lose your job if you did. Only quite a few leader writers are amusing.

It may be your lot to write the kind of extra leader which some papers have. This must be On Something, it does not much matter what, so long as it is not connected with current events, but you must write in a gentle, musing, good-humoured style, and if you are cross about anything you must not say so.

Now let us suppose for a moment that you are, in-

stead, a reporter.    Reporters have not to comment, but
to report.    They are sent out by News Editors, each
after a separate story.    You must remember, if you are
a reporter, that you must return to your office with the
story you were sent out to get, however many others
you may collect as you go about.    However, if some
other amazing scene than that which you have been
sent out to view should meet your eye by the way, you
can certainly make a note of it and submit it.    In this
connection, you should remember that everything which
occurs is News if you and the news editor like to make
it so.    No day need be a news-less day.    The daily
round, the common task, will furnish all you need to
ask.    Thus, even if you cannot truthfully report a
crime, a street accident, a divorce, or a fall of the Prince
of Wales from his horse, you can always say, "Amazing Crowds in Oxford Street" (or at some railway
station, or anywhere else where people congregate)
"Scenes."    You may, in fact, report anything you like,
provided that you report it in the right spirit, with the
correct amount of élan, gusto, and amaze.    News is
like food; it is the cooking and serving that makes it
acceptable, not the material itself.    You should, before
you can hope to succeed as a reporter, have a course in
Journalese.    (Hugo's *Journalese in Twelve Lessons
without a Master* will be found a useful handbook.    The
Berlitz system is also a good one.)

A course of this language will also be found useful
if your job is that of literary, dramatic, or artistic
critic.    You must learn to call certain books or plays

"important," even though you cannot see how any book or play can possibly be important. You may also say "convincing" (or unconvincing, as the case may more likely be) instead of crudely saying that the thing is well or badly done. You will also find "gripping," which is journalese for interesting, a useful word.

If you are a practised reviewer of fiction, you will very soon learn to divide the books you have to review into quite a few categories according to their subjects. Thus, they may deal with Family Life, Village Life, London Life, Married Life, Individual Life, School Life, American Life, Corpses, International Conspiracies, South Sea Islands, or Love. As you will not wish to read the books, I will set down a few hints as to what to say of each class. Family Life and Village Life are both rather sad, disagreeable subjects. The people who live in families and villages are seldom good or at all nice to one another. Villages are the worst, for they are imbecile as well as criminal. They go further than families, as families only think and speak criminally, and villagers act. You may safely call a Village Life novel realistic and powerful, even, in some cases, sordid. If you call a Family Life novel any of these, you will probably be going further than the text warrants, and may be sued for libel. London Life novels are much gayer. They deal, as a rule, with London. You may say, if you like, that they are about well-known society figures, many of whom will be easily recognisable to their friends and enemies. London Life novels are not realistic, powerful, or sordid, as people in London have a wider range of entertainment and are therefore more cheerful. Besides, novels about persons who pay income tax are not realistic. And persons who pay super-tax are not considered by most reviewers real people at all. Novels about Married Life are often "poignant studies of a very modern problem" (à propos, you will find much of what you need to say kindly supplied for you by the publisher on the paper wrapper. But you must not trust blurb-writers too implicitly, for they have not, any more than you, read the book about which they blurb; I once read a blurb which thought the brigand villain was a horse). Stories of School Life are a little *passée* now. But, should one come your way, you can safely say that it deals once more with the problems of adolescence from a realistic angle, and that nothing is shirked, though Mr. —— is always restrained.

American Life may be divided into sub-sections. There are novels about Eastern America, or civilised life (perhaps by Mrs. Wharton or Miss Sedgwick), Middle Western Life (which you should praise), Wild Western Life (which are about cow-boys or long white trails, and published by Messrs. Hodder and Stoughton), and South American Life (which I recommend you to read, as they are probably readable).

Novels about Corpses are often readable, too. For the corpse, you should look in the library, in one of the early chapters, and there you will find the murdered body of an elderly gentleman. It is safe to say of this book that the mystery is well kept to the end (or else that you spotted the murderer straight off, according as you wish well or ill to the author) and that there is a happy affair between the detective, or the suspected but innocent young man (you had better ascertain which), and the corpse's niece, daughter, or ward (you need not ascertain which).

Novels about International Conspiracies deal with Bolshevists, and relate world-wide schemes for the overthrow of established governments and the setting up of a world dominion. You will quite soon see if a book is about this. You may safely say that the Bolshevists are bad men, and that their schemes are defeated by the intrepid hero.

Books about South Sea Islands reveal themselves at once. If you open them anywhere, you will see "yam," "bread-fruit," "palm toddy," "kanaka," "beachcomber," or "lagoon." You can call them picturesque, romantic, or exciting, or (if you feel more like it) "cheap lagoonery."

Books above Love deal with a well-worn subject in a new and moving way.

Some reviewers like to be quoted by publishers in advertisements; others are shy, and do not. If you do, you should make your favourable comments detachable from the context; thus, if you desire to express distaste and yet be quoted, you may say "This cannot be called a really good book," and trust that the publishers may know which words to select. If you do *not* like being quoted, you should be careful to express any favourable views you may hold in a delicate and obscure way which shall elude the publisher's grasp, and see you do not hang your laudations like cullable blossoms on a bough.

In reviewing, you should try to sound more intelligent than you are, and never fall back on saying "I like this book, it seems to me interesting, and the kind of book I like." Proper reviewers never write like this.

Nor do proper dramatic critics. It is very nice to be a dramatic critic, and you must get that job if you can, but there are not nearly enough of them to go round, so you probably won't. It is a nice job because you get a free stall for the first or second nights of plays, and having to think of something to say about the play (and getting paid for saying it) is a small price to pay for this. You may even enjoy expressing your views on the play. Everyone has views on the plays that they have seen, and mentioning them is not at all difficult. It does not matter whether you mention them well or ill, for scarcely anyone will read you. (This applies also to criticisms of books.) I say *scarcely* anyone, because your comments will be eagerly perused by the whole cast of the play, as well as by the author, manager, and producer. But be sure you will have no effect on the general public, who know better than to believe you. So you can say just what you like (unless you are friends with the author, manager, producer, or some of the cast). It is thought better form if somewhere in the course of your notice you deplore the present inferiority of the English stage, and lament that in England there is no national theatre, which means a theatre run by the Government. Members of the Government like this to be done, as they do not receive many compliments on their artistic talents. It is usual also to mention that one or another of the actresses has beauty, even if she cannot act; actresses like this. It is not, for some reason, so customary to comment on the beauty of actors, though they too like it.

If you do not wish to be out of line with the other critics, there is no reason why you should be, as it is customary for the critics to meet together between the acts in the refreshment room and decide together what to say. If, on the other hand, you wish to be original, you should join these gatherings all the same, so that you will know what not to say. It is really better to be original, just at first, as it gives an impression that you have thought for yourself. But you must remember that it is better form to admire the plays of other dramatic critics, as you never know when you may not write a play yourself; most critics do. Then, if you have got on the wrong side of the other critics by crabbing their plays, where are you? There is a good deal of give and take in matters of criticism.

On some first nights you must say that the audience was brilliant. Especially you can say this of a Sunday play, which other actors and actresses often attend. No one knows how an audience shows its brilliance, and whether the word refers to clothes, wits, or social eminence, but it probably means merely "heard of before." Anyhow, if short of remarks to make about the play, you can thus comment on the audience, who, if they should chance to read you, will be pleased.

So much for critics, on the whole a not very well thought of race. It pays better to be a serial story writer. But it is even more difficult to get this job, for it is at least a thousand to one against any paper accepting you in this capacity. You should aim first at the well-got-up, glossy monthlies, for these pay best, but I fear you will have no luck with them, for they like what is called a Name, and I am assuming that your name is not a Name. Less ambitious are the dailies; but even these will probably reject anything you write. There are two necessary ingredients in a daily serial—love and a synopsis. If you cannot manage both of these, you may as well renounce serial ambitions and take to some other branch of journalism, such as Personal Notes. These are much easier. They consist of little items of information about persons supposedly known to the public, such as "Mr. ——, whose friends know him as 'Nicky,' has recently returned from a trip to the South Seas," or "Miss ——, the novelist, tall, and with delicately arched black brows, tells me that she writes five hours a day in her lovely country home at Beckenham." You can, if you like, call on your victims and seek an interview, asking them who are their greatest friends, what in their lives has most deeply influenced them, and what they think of the Oxford trousers. If by these means you annoy some persons, they cannot easily avenge themselves, and if you please them it is well.

If you write the Woman's Page, you must learn about face creams, foods, and furniture polish, for these are what women like. You must learn to write like this: "Dear Dot, what *do* you think Betty and I saw in Marshall's yesterday? The dinkiest little boudoir cap, shaped like a convolvulus flower and trimmed with point de Venise." You must keep in close touch with the advertisement department, and mention by name those firms whose advertisement your paper desires, as "I had the loveliest face massage yesterday from Mrs. ——, in Bond Street. I've never before had 'that fresh feeling' so marvellously. Every woman ought to go." Mrs. —— will then send in an advertisement for next week's issue, and the advertisement department will thank you.

But the best journalistic job is that of Foreign Correspondent. For this you live in some pleasant foreign city, with a suitable entertainment allowance as well as your salary, and have a very good time (unless you are unfortunate enough to be sent to Russia). You can send home any news you like, for no one will know whether or not you are telling the truth. You must by all means be this kind of journalist if you can.

We have dealt thus at large, though by no means exhaustively, with various problems of journalism, because we are convinced that it is an important profession, and that the Fourth Estate, as it has been well called, should be upheld by all who desire their country's good. Ephemeral the productions of this estate may and indeed must be. But let them be flowers that bloom beautifully, and give out a sweet fragrance ere they perish.   Those who hold that the only use of the press is to lay the fires and line drawers, give it, I think, too low a place in the scheme of things.   For it also serves to keep moths from clothes, these little creatures having, it is said, a great and unreasonable distaste for printer's ink.

# PROBLEMS OF A DOCTOR'S LIFE

THE profession of healing is a very noble one, and you should be a doctor if you can. Do not, on any account, be a nurse. Nurses get very little pay and a great deal of work. Doctors get more money (when they get any) than nurses, and do less work. If you should succeed in obtaining access to the house of any sick person (a doubtful hypothesis, of course) you can pay as many visits as you like, and charge seven and sixpence, or even half a guinea, for each. If you should ever be so fortunate as to induce any sick persons, or persons believing themselves to be sick, to visit your house instead, you may charge a great deal more, since this will be far less trouble to you, and the general rule applies to medicine, as to other professions (e.g., the literary profession, in which the printers do all the hard work, and the author and publisher get the most money)—the less the work the higher the pay. But (I say it without wish to insult) you are not likely to reach this eminence. You can, indeed, sit in your house and put a notice on your street door to the effect that you have consulting hours, but you cannot, unfortunately, compel anyone to come in. Should, however, this agreeable event occur, you should not be so astonished as to be taken unawares; you should be ready for the emergency. You should have a stethoscope, and apply one end to the patient and the other to your ear with some appearance of habit; it does not matter which end you apply to each, as neither you nor the patient will probably be any the wiser. You should never listen in vain; always hear something through your stethoscope, the murmur of some still small voice. While listening, it is well to nod or shake the head once or twice, with an appearance of comprehension or disapproval, or both. Having removed the instrument, you will tell the patient a little of his or her condition, with an air of restraint, as of one who withholds the worst. You will prescribe something, it matters little what (as you must describe it, for the chemist's perusal, in a series of symbols in abbreviated Latin, your patient need never know what it is) ; and bid him return in a week. When he says, "For how much am I indebted to you?" or "How much is that?" according to the elegance or otherwise of his manners, you should inform him that the sum is five guineas (you should not at first charge more), but that subsequent visits will be only three. Expensiveness sends up a doctor's stock. So also does mystery; a doctor should be a magic-man. It is said that there was once a doctor at a hospital who, in a prescription, wrote "water" instead of "aq." The rumour of this lapse into lucidity went round, and he was dismissed from the hospital and never had a patient. Doctors must never descend to the common level from the misty heights on which they stand. In our hearts we, the public, know that doctors do not know much more than we do ourselves about what ails us, but it would never do to have this admitted, or faith, that great element in the healing of the sick, would perish.

At first, if you are a doctor, you had better be a general practitioner—as general as the public will allow you to be. But soon it will be well to specialise, as you will earn more that way, and need to know even less. You can specialise in any organ of the human frame, which is so fortunately constructed (from a doctor's point of view) that all its organs are more often sick than well. Thus, you may specialise in hearts, lungs, livers, kidneys, appendices, brains, nerves, legs, arms, stomachs, eyes, ears, throats, blood, bones, or complexes. In Edwardian days appendices were the most fashionable subject to take up; a few years ago it was complexes; just now it is bones. The osteopath has succeeded the psychoanalyst with the best people. If you are an osteopath, you tell your patient, whatever his disease may be, that what he needs is to have all his bones taken apart and restrung. If he consents, you must then do this. The important thing is to remember how the bones went before you unstrung them, and put them together in a new way; it is the opposite to putting a watch together again, and easier, as new ways are many and the old way only one. So you ought to have very little trouble over this. But some people prefer to specialise in something that they do not have to take to pieces at all, such as hearts. Hearts only need listening to. When you have listened, you mention what you might have heard, had you heard anything, and tell the patient that he may last, with care, for some years, but, without care, for only as many weeks, since his heart is not one to be played tricks with. As he knew that before, and, indeed, it is a statement true of all hearts, he will believe you, and thank you for being so candid with him.

But it is possibly more entertaining and profitable to be a brain specialist. The human heart is a poor enough organ, but the human brain is still poorer. There is no brain but needs attention and a drastic course of treatment. Unfortunately, however, it is only a small proportion of brains which realise this, or, anyhow, which believe that medical treatment will remedy the matter. Some prefer Pelman. However, there are always (and especially in these cross-word days of ours) some brain patients whose relatives bring them to a brain specialist, and should you be fortunate enough to meet with such, your course is easy. Do not attempt to take the brain to pieces, as it needs more skill to put it together again than the bones do, and nearly as much as a watch. It is simpler to pronounce the patient mad and order him to a private asylum. As most people are rather mad and should be in asylums, you need have no scruples about this. If ever the patient gets out, he may possibly sue you for damages, but you will get the best of him in the end. Even if you do not, and have to pay damages which you do not recover on appeal, which is unlikely, you will have made so considerable a sum out of the gratitude of the asylum that you will still be the gainer.

As to other organs of the human body and mind, such as eyes, ears, liver, appendix, lungs, nerves, limbs, complexes, teeth, and so on, you should encourage your patients to follow the Biblical maxim, and cut them off or pluck them out. I know a doctor who only has one prescription for all ills. "Have," he says, "all the teeth extracted. I perceive that they are poisoning your system." As a regular response to this admonition, a patient of his whom I know plucks, with an easy gesture, his complete artificial denture from his mouth and displays it. When this occurs to you, do not be disconcerted, but remark that badly made artificial teeth are often more poisonous than real ones. It is safe to recommend the removal of almost any organ, except possibly the heart and brain.

If no one comes to consult you, you must buy, or otherwise acquire, a practice, and become a general practitioner. The drawbacks to general practice are (*a*) babies, who are born with considerable frequency, and usually at very inconvenient times for you, (*b*) being called up in the night, (*c*) the disagreeable atmosphere of some of the sick-rooms into which you may have to penetrate.

You will perhaps be happier if you remain in a hospital, where the nurses have to stand while you are in the room and hold basins for you to wash in. You will never be so much admired after you leave hospital, for, in the world at large, though you will be in request, you will always meet with a certain amount of disagreeable scepticism, and some ungrateful people will always be ready to say, "Thou that art doctor of death, drynk that thou madest"—which would be a very unpleasant thing to have to do.

It is less trouble to be a Faith Healer. These have to know even less than doctors of medicine. The only thing they have to know is that a certain number of people can and will believe anything they are told.

# PROBLEMS OF A WRITER'S LIFE

WE all have our troubles, our little crosses to bear, as the hymn puts it. The primary trouble in the life of a writer is, of course, writing. Any form of work is insufferably tedious, and this not least (though assuredly not most, either). You cannot get round or escape this trouble; in the long run, defer it as you may, you will find that the law at last holds good: writers must write. They need not write much, and very certainly they need not write well, but a little something now and then they must produce, or they will, as the phrase is, go under. Very likely they will go under in any case, but this is more honourably done (if you are a writer) by writing than by abstaining from writing.

So, every now and then, the writer has to pull herself (or himself, but on the whole male writers seem to be more industrious, less inert of habit, knowing that men must toil) together, sit down with pen and paper (or typewriter, which is much worse, as it demands more concentration and a more upright position) and Write. It is a frightful compulsion. For what has to be produced is not mere agreeable dalliance, mere unthinking self-expression, with the pen instead

of the tongue as medium, as was the pleasant habit of
our childhood. Over all that we now write hangs the
shadow of an awful doom: it will Come Out. It will
appear, in cold print (print is, we are informed, of
low temperature—not that this makes appearing in it
any worse) and make a fool of us in the eyes of all
who run and read. Many (perhaps most) of these will
be our valued friends. Others will be Reviewers.
These, perhaps, will not care for what we write, and
will say so. They are paid to do this, and we cannot
blame them. Indeed, we are probably of them, for
many writers are also reviewers, and know well the
troubles of that foolish, prejudiced, fanciful, well-in-
tentioned band, whose trade it is to invent thoughts
about books which stir them to no thoughts at all, nor
could, who are smothered, pile upon pile, by a night-
mare of frightful volumes. For, whatever you may
think of an exception here and there, books in the
main *are* frightful: there is no doubt about it.

This is a digression. I was speaking of the awful
doom of print which awaits the written or the typed
word. But there is a worse doom than getting into
print—not getting into print. The manuscript may go
forth from the writer to return with a faithfulness
passing the faithfulness of the boomerang or the hom-
ing pigeon. This is one of the heaviest troubles in a
writer's life. Well may he wonder, was he born for
this—to write and write, and never to be read? He
does not demand to be a best seller; he does not even
demand a *succès d'estime,* or that critics should call

him clever. But he would like, he would very much like, just to be in print, so that those could read him who might so· wish.

Print. Those dear little neat black letters, so different from the letters produced by the pen, or even by the typewriter. Never to get there! The bitter frustration of that closed door! What fearful complexes, psychoanalysts would doubtless tell us, are produced by that frustration, that suppression! It may well be that it is responsible for a larger number of the world's crimes than is generally supposed. For, though writers are very many, non-writers (or rather, non-publishers) are even more numerous. How many decoy telegrams, how many forged cheques, are writ‹ ten by those who would fain be writing newspaper articles or books, but cannot achieve either, so fall back on these lesser branches of the art!

But these are, perhaps, not strictly the troubles of a writer's life. As has been said, the chief of these is Writing. For, indeed, what can be written that is worth writing? Nothing, if one uses "worth" to denote such ultimate standard of eternal value. If, on the other hand, by "worth" one means worth (or any‹ how productive of) money, then much writing falls into this category. Many novels, for instance.

Novels are among the queerest things in a queer world. Chunks out of the imagined life of a set of imagined persons, set down for others to read. For this is what you have to produce if you are a novelist. You will find it quite easy. Anyone can write novels, and most people, at one time or another, do so. One novel is much like another, so you need not worry very much about what kind of novel to write. Take up your pen, and you may be sure that something will flow out of its nib, even if it be only ink. The great advantage of writing novels is that some people read novels. They are not, on the while, very clever people, so yours need not be clever novels, and, indeed, had better not be. You may be sure that someone will tell you, in print, that it is clever, whatever it is like, for reviewers are very kind, and like to pay compliments, unless any of them have a private grudge against you, which they will, if you write a book, be happy to pay. You need not mind what reviews say, for they are not much read except by you and your publishers. But you must make your publishers say, often and conspicuously, in the public press (and, if possible, in tube lifts) that your book exists and has sold many copies, for if the general public are told this loudly and often, they hasten to read it; they do not mind whether or not it is good, so long as they believe that many others have read it. You must, therefore, make friends with your publisher and get him to proclaim you well. He should, for instance, in public announcements, always add a nought to the number of copies he has sold of your book, so that five hundred has the air of being five thousand, and so forth.

For the rest, all you have to do is to think of something to write about. You should first decide whether you are going to try to please yourself or your readers. You will probably, of course, do neither; and you may be lucky enough to do both; but sometimes there seems to be a choice. You may have reason to believe, for instance, that your novel will be more pleasing to the majority if you introduce that curious thing known as "a love interest." You may be personally bored by the thought of introducing this interest, of treading such a familiar path; you may desire to confine yourself to adventure, conversation, crime, food, or drink. But you will, if wise, exercise compulsion on yourself; you will set your teeth and say: "The people in my novel shall find time, among their avocations, to love. They shall desist from talking, eating, preaching, committing crimes, and shall feel one for the other that acute emotion we call sexual affection. They shall not only feel this, but they shall mention it, even discuss it; they shall take action on account of it; they shall give the subject their attention." For this, you must remember, is what numbers of people like to read about. Probably because everyone knows about it from personal experience, and was, naturally, intensely moved by it when it entered his or her own life. And, indeed, it is the most moving of human experiences; though anything less moving than its treatment by very nearly all novelists can scarcely be imagined. But anyhow it is familiar, and puts no strain on the reader's imagination; whatever he does not know, he knows about that. And a strange penchant for the familiar seems to obsess many readers. Criminals (one is told) like to read about crime, gourmands about meals, business men about financial intrigues, children about school.

But the writer, on the other hand, often prefers to write about the unfamiliar, the strange; he prefers to describe life on tropic islands, long-laid schemes for revenge, elaborate and improbable intrigues, or those shades of feeling which are more subtle, more improbable, less universally felt, than the primary and elementary emotions. He finds it more interesting to write of odd persons in odder situations, treading paths not as a rule, possibly never, trodden, by actual human beings. On the other hand, he may desire to write of life as lived and be quite unable to do so. Novelists, even when they are trying their hardest to be realistic, are as a rule strangely the reverse, for between life as lived and life as recorded stands the muddled brain and impotent pen of the recorder.

Readers do not know how hard even the most improbable novelist may have tried to be truthful; he has difficulties to contend with that they know not of. He no doubt knows well enough how life—some life, that is—is actually lived, but his lips are sealed: he cannot tell. So he gabbles away in his infinitely strange system of symbols, which bear, except in his mind (and often not in that), no relation whatsoever to actual conversation, actual happenings, actual emotions. Let it pass for a record: truth, after all, is relative, and no one sees it but as through a glass darkly.

Anyhow, you will enjoy being a novelist, for it is very little trouble, and, to write novels, you need no preliminary education.

To be a dramatist is less satisfactory, for though

anyone can write a play, it is less easy to make money out of it, since the managers of theatres are very particular as to what they stage. You may easily get your play acted on a Sunday evening by the Stage Society or some other private enterprise, but one performance will not help you much financially. What you want is a run, and this is what you will not, in all probability, get. There are no rules in this game, for it is on the knees of the manager and play-goer, and these two are mysterious creatures, whom no one has yet understood. They do not even understand one another. The manager spends his time trying to understand the play-goer, and the play-goer a little of his in dismissing the manager as beyond comprehension. The dramatic critic, who is the average play-goer turned loose to express himself in print, tries to explain the play-goer's point of view to the manager, but it is very difficult to explain, and they get no nearer one another. Still, sometimes they click, and then a play runs. Sometimes this occurs to a good play, sometimes to a bad; as I said, there are no rules in this game, and you had better not try to play it.

One can well imagine that others, looking at a writer's life from the outside, may cry: "Troubles of a writer! These idle wielders of the pen, they have no troubles. Let them but for a day be clerks, bricklayers, doctors, nurses, bankers, lawyers, schoolmasters, cooks, policemen, or bishops, and they would soon know what trouble was. Theirs but idly to scribble foolish words, for which they receive excessive pay. They do not even have to do their work decently well. If a doctor diagnosed, if a banker banked, if a builder built, if a lawyer drew up a deed, if a cook cooked, if a dustman conveyed dust, as badly as these make books —what failure, what penury would be theirs! But the makers of bad books are often richly rewarded, gaining much money, or the applause of multitudes. Speak not to us of a writer's troubles."

And, indeed, one scarcely likes to do so. It is an inequitable world. Possibly in another the writers will be condemned to some hard, tedious, and gritty labour, and the bankers, the builders, the dustmen, the bishops, and the cooks will have to write. . . .

All the same, let these be warned, a writer's life is not all jam. Besides the primary and heavy trouble of having to write, and the even heavier trouble of being neither published nor paid, his life contains many incidental griefs. He will, for instance, be asked from time to time to do things which he has no taste for, such as helping with bazaars, contributing to anthologies, speaking in public, writing articles on subjects which do not please him. He may, in his folly, if the date of delivery is a long way ahead, say he will do it, supposing that the time will never come, for he may die first, or the world may end, or it may please God to take him to whom he has made the promise. But, alas! none of these things occur; inevitably the date does come, and with it a reminder of the obligation contracted; and this is a heavy trouble indeed.

Strange, inquisitive questions are asked of the writer.

Newspapers will ask him whether poetry is a necessity of life, whether he approves of marriage, how many hours he works a day, how he invents his characters, what is his favourite cocktail, and so on and so forth. Often a stamped envelope is enclosed, or even a reply-paid telegram, and then the writer, unless he is willing to make a fool of himself in a newspaper, is haunted by the thought of all this money expended on him for no return. . . .

Or, on the other hand, all the other writers may be asked for their views on these topics and not he, and then he will feel mortified. For the human heart is full of vanity, and not least the heart of the writer.

Having written thus far, I pause to consider. And it occurs to me that I had better stop, for, if all a writer's troubles should be set down, I suppose that the world itself would not contain all the books that would be filled therewith. But then this same observation applies to every trade under the sun. For man is born to trouble as the sparks fly upward.

## PROBLEMS OF A READER'S LIFE

SINCE, some fifty years ago, that minimum of education which included learning to read became compulsorily inflicted on an all too patient people, the members of this nation have been great and irrational readers. Truly the human race finds its pleasure in odd ways, and one of the oddest is the absorption of ideas from black marks imprinted on white paper. Everywhere you go you shall see the British race, intent and absorbed, with something of the vacant imbecility of countenance of the drug-taker, pouring over these black marks, deriving from them imagined narratives of fiction or of fact, putting themselves wise as to which horse has excelled other horses in trials of skill and of speed, which fighter with his fists has used these to best advantage, what has been said or done by the more loquacious and active of our statesmen, which countries have gone to war, what murders have been perpetrated, what marriages annulled, and, in general, which of the world's follies have been held suitable for recording by the press. Or they will be perusing less ephemeral literature, between cloth covers —imaginary tales, essays, scientific discourses, even verse. It may truly be said that there is nothing printed which someone will not read, all too patient (as I re-marked above) people that we are.

Foreigners are different. They do not read so much. Their imaginations are more self-sufficient and their print less good.

Some readers, I believe, do not greatly care what they read, and, indeed, scarcely know. For these fortunate ones, the problems of a reader's life are few. Other readers—and these are a very rational class, with whom I have every sympathy—dislike reading anything, though they cannot wholly avoid it. For these the problem is simple—how to avoid as much of it as possible. There is a third and larger class, which likes reading some things and not others. It is for these that the problems of a reader's life mainly arise. What to read; how to select, from the masses of as yet unread literature which pours forth daily from the printing presses, such matter as will please; this is the problem in chief.

If you are very cautious, you will take no risks, but confine yourself to literature already read and liked in your less cautious past. But I surmise that you are not so careful as to do this; you want at times to read something which you have not read before. It is a laudable enterprise, and one as a rule ill rewarded. For, there is no manner of doubt about it, most books, most journals, are a great pity, and will not please you, unless you are very easily pleased indeed. You will suffer heavily in your search after agreeable reading matter. Many a book, many a newspaper, many a periodical, you will weary of before it is well begun. In the case of periodicals, this matters little, perhaps, since these are not costly and can be sampled and thrown aside with ease. But books are a different affair. To obtain a book to read, you have perhaps made an expedition, comfortless and tiresome, to a library; even, possibly (but this is rash, and a thing I personally should not care to do), you may have purchased the book with money. Anyhow, time for reading is short, in most lives, and it is sad waste to expend it on the wrong books. How, then, may we know beforehand, and by exterior evidence, if a book will please us or not?

There are several ways. The merits of literature are seldom hidden under bushels; they are, as a rule, proclaimed in public places by those who have detected them. You have but to open any daily and weekly papers to see high praise in large and bold type, spaced off in enclosures, of many a score of books. If you can believe these ejaculations of applause, your only problem is how many of these works of genius you can get read in the brief span of life yet remaining to you. If you are more sceptical, and yet not so much so as to reject the opinions of others altogether, you can read those printed opinions known as *reviews*. You will not agree with these after you have read the books, but you may do so beforehand, and, as they are often complimentary, your problem as to which books to select is only slightly narrowed. From reviews you would gather that there is a considerable output of good literature every day. If you do not want to be disappointed, it is better not to trust reviews too much. You must remember that reviewers, like you, are human, and, again like you, kindly, and that many of their friends write books; like you, also, they have not much time for reading, and, if you have not time to read a book, it is only just to praise it. I do not mean that all reviewers praise all books; books are written not only by the friends of reviewers, and reviewers, like you, are sometimes out of temper, or do not like the author or publisher, or what not; besides which, they have their moments of real distaste for a book, and in some cases they will not hesitate to mention this, particularly if the writer be of small importance. But, be the reviewer scornful, or approving, the odds are that you will not agree with him. You must make your selection some other way.

First, it is well to decide whether you prefer to read poetry, history, science, essays, biography, travel, fiction, or the newspapers. Let us suppose for a moment that your brain is not very highly developed, and that you are only up to the two latter branches of literature. We will first, then, consider fiction. Many persons read and like fiction. It does not tax the intelligence, and the intelligence of most of us can so ill afford taxation that we rightly welcome any reading matter which avoids this. Those who enjoy reading fiction are, you may say, well provided for, seeing that several hundred works of fiction appear weekly in this country alone. And, indeed, readers of small discrimination and contented nature should be quite content. But one novel differs often (though not always) from another novel, and some prefer one, some another. Some readers will only read detective stories. These persons are quite in the fashion just now, but unfortunate, for there is a good deal of moderation in the writing of detective stories, and very often you will only find two or three new ones in a week. You should be a little cautious in your selection of what you believe to be detective novels, for you may easily be misled by a deceptive title or a beguiling picture on the paper jacket; I have known cases of those who thought they saw a picture of a gentleman murdering a lady by throttling, when really he was but embracing her, and found themselves landed with a milk-and-water love story when they had hoped for crime. Neither should you always think that such a name as "The Mystery of Beach House" or the like necessarily indicates crime; there are other mysteries in the world besides murder, and not all mysteries are interesting. No; unless you get an unmistakable name such as "Who Killed Smith?" you would be wise to look inside before taking the book out of the library, or else to ask the probably well-informed assistant who serves you, and who, you will find, has read every novel that comes into the library. If you look inside for yourself, look at the middle chapters, but not at the last few pages, which will probably be devoted to the completion of the love affair between the hero and the niece or daughter of the murdered, and will therefore tell you nothing material. And be careful only to glance, just so as to assure yourself that it is the right stuff, or you may discover by mistake who committed the crime, which would spoil the book.

Possibly, on the other hand, you do not care for detective stories. After all, why should you? You may well feel (as I do) that if a man's dead he's dead, and there's an end of it, and what does it matter who killed him? For my part, I greatly prefer a tale of a man who is not dead yet, but who soon may be, if the gang of international crooks who are on his track get half a chance with him. You ought, without much trouble, to be able to discover whether or no a novel is about this. Or perhaps you prefer a Wild West narrative, called the Long, Lone, White, Great, Wild, or something else Trail, and with a picture on the wrapper of persons in buckskins, with broncos or guns. I do not think that you can make a mistake about these. As a rule they are by Mr. Ottwell Binns, though others weigh in from time to time.

Or do you like something quieter, more domestic, about family life, with a nice love story? For this I should recommend Mr. D. H. Lawrence, or Miss May Sinclair. But several of our novelists do this well. Or you may like novels about Sussex, or South Sea Islands, or Russia, or about the career of a serious young man from the cradle onwards, or the career of a young woman, less serious, in London, Paris, or Budapest. Or (which is quite in the mode among intelligent novelists) an account of one week, day, hour, or minute in a quiet life. Or (which has always been in the mode among somewhat less intelligent novelists) womanly novels about true love did not run smooth but at last came right. Old-fashioned novelists used often to lay the scene of these in a desert, and to make the hero a fierce and cruel man armed with a dog-whip, but this is now gone out. However, the idea is the same —that Love Wins Out. If, by some chance, you cannot read these novels, your problem will be how to avoid them.

But why all this bother as to what novels are about? It does not, after all, matter. A novel on any theme may be witty, graceful, charming, or interesting. A novel on any theme may be the reverse of all these things. It quite often is; that is the trouble. Whether it be about crime, love, psychology, international crooks, desert islands, family life, great white trails, politics, finance, young women or young men, the same heavy, witless touch is usually brought to bear on it, kneading it into the dull mass of dough that lies in piles on the library table, repelling our investigations. And the great problem for the novel reader is to discover the exceptions. These exist, but how few and far between! Each reader has to find his or her own, since all tastes differ. There is no guide beyond acquaintance with the previous works of the writers you are considering, and even that is not infallible. No; this is a thankless quest in the dark, and its rewards are few. Perhaps it is better to bear all novels with equanimity, or else to read none of them, but to turn your attention to other branches of literature, such as newspapers. These are even more numerous than novels. You cannot possibly hope to read all the newspapers every day. You will have to select. You had better not try to read any of them all through, as there is a great deal in newspapers which is above your head, such as the City news. The two outside pages of the *Times* you can strip off at once and use for some purpose other than literary. Even what is left you had better not try to read through. You will find, on the whole, that the penny papers are more within your scope, and particularly the evening ones, which may be procured hourly from ten a.m. onwards until six. It is quite important that you should read these, as they contain a great deal of news that you will not see again in the morning. Having first ascertained that the horse you backed did nothing, you can proceed to the account of some game played with balls, and then to the day's record of murders, crimes, entertainments, divorces, international disputes, motor accidents, and traffic jams. You will find these papers far more varied and interesting reading than most novels. The only drawback to this form of literature is that there is so much of it that it may well take all your time and all your money, besides filling your home with more paper than is needed for the fires or to line drawers with. The best plan is to spend your days at your club, where you may see all the papers free of charge. You must remember to read papers of all shades of thought, or you may develop a biassed mind, as newspapers are apt to be opinionated. You should always believe all you read in newspapers, as this makes them more interesting. By the end of each day your mind will thus be a storehouse of occurrences, and you will be able to hold your own very well at dinner-time and pass as a much-informed man or woman.

If you do not care for either novels or newspapers, you can try biography, poetry, drama, essays, or those books mysteriously classed as belles-lettres. Most of these also are bad, but they are not quite so numerous as newspapers and novels. You should be careful about poetry, as this is often poor. However, there is not very much of it written just now; our poetical output has greatly diminished in bulk since the end of the great war. There are only quite a few living poets who write good poetry. It is safer to read dead ones, as only a few of these have been suffered to survive in print. As to most modern plays, these should not be read, but only seen, if that. Memoirs, essays, and travels may be amusing or (more probably) may not. Those who write of their travels are sadly apt to be discursive, and to give their private opinions, whereas all we want of them is an account of the places they saw, the inns that put them up, and the best ways to get from place to place. Guide-books make the best reading. But there are no perfect guide-books; they are all spoilt by something. Methuen's Little Guides, for instance, would be excellent reading, but the writers nearly all tell you details about the font or piscina in the church when you want to know what the village **is** like. Also, they say "quaint." And Baedeker keeps plunging, for no apparent reason, into small print. However, in spite of these faults, and in spite of the priggish style in which the authors of guide-books write, guide-books make, on the whole, the best reading.

Always excepting the Oxford Dictionary. If you can manage to lift one of the volumes of this from its shelf, you will find it the best reading of all, infinitely varied in its contents, and full of elegant and brief extracts from the English literature of all times.

Having solved, in however rough, ready and unsatisfactory a fashion, the problem of what to read, it next remains to be considered how and where and when to read it. The ideal reading-place (only not for the Oxford Dictionary) is, of course, the bed. If you wish to get much reading done, you should go to bed early and rise late. Only one hour in the normal day is more pleasurable than the hour spent in bed with a book before going to sleep, and that is the hour spent in bed with a book after being called in the morning. The more loudly and clearly conscience, that brainless alarm clock, summons us to rise and begin the so-called duties of the day (duties often better left unfulfilled), the more deeply and exquisitely we shall enjoy that morning hour. We may not succeed in stealing from the miserly day so much as a whole hour; but, be it only a few minutes, they are divine minutes and should be savoured to the full. For toil the day was given, for rest the night, as the hymn says; it should, then, be our object to prolong as far as may be the hours of rest, and to fill them with pleasure. It does not, perhaps, greatly matter, in this exquisite hour, what you read; words, words, words; almost any of these will do. In the peace and joy of bed (even, who knows, of early tea) small discriminations between one book and another will be found to vanish away and any reading matter serves.

Failing bed, books may be read in trains, omnibuses, or offices. Or, of course, after the day's work is done, sitting in an arm-chair by a fire. Or, in summer weather, out of doors. I have known those who read walking or bicycling. But this habit seems to show a rather morbid avidity for the printed word, and the best people, I believe, devote themselves while exercising to the study only of that book which who runs may read, and of such books as they discover in the running brooks. And the still better people do not even do this, but throw off, while out, all thoughts of literature, and become as the exploring dog or the browsing beasts of the fields.

There was a time when, to my infant mind, the problem of a reader's life was how to find time, however old I may live to be, to read all the books in the world. My point of view had sadly changed. For now, should all the books in the world be laid before me, my problem would be how many of them I could avoid. Most books are like that.

## PROBLEMS OF SOCIAL LIFE

THERE is an American book on Etiquette being much advertised just now, price two dollars, which professes to teach us all how to live. Would you like to know, inquires the advertisement of this book, how to dress, how to have perfect table-manners, whether to eat asparagus with a fork or fingers (I gather that the answer is with a fork, so one should be careful not to rely overmuch on this book in Great Britain), how to create conversation, how to order at a restaurant, how to avoid impulsive blunders at the dance, how to be calm and at ease wherever you go? The book is, apparently, adorned with intriguing illustrations, representing groups of persons, one or more (perhaps all) of whom are doing the Wrong Thing, behaving as if they were not used to Good Society. What mistake or mistakes are these people making? the legend under the picture runs. I regret to say that I do not think I have guessed the riddle in any of these pictures; the mistakes are too subtle for me. I can only see that they all look very vulgar and very self-conscious, and obviously have not yet bought the Book, and attained thereby to that repose that stamps the caste of Vere de Vere.

I have in my own possession a small English book, which must be, I think, a reprint from an early Vic-

torian work, called *Correct Conduct.* It is very edify-
ing reading. It is the correct thing, according to this
book, to look upon your morning bath as a duty to
yourself and to society; to appear in the morning fully
equipped, but in a totally different style from that of
the evening; at breakfast, to choose what is already on
the table unless it is positively disagreeable to you; at
lunch, to make a sufficient but light meal, and not to
conduct yourself as if you were dining or taking your
one heavy meal of the day; at dinner, to remember that
this is the repast *par excellence,* and to treat it as such
in every respect; to appear to be pleased with your
dinner-partner, as you have no means of escaping from
the *tête-à-tête;* to eat and drink judiciously; to regard
your pocket-handkerchief, when you are in society, as
an article of ornament, not of use (whether you should
use your sleeve, or what, the book does not say); and
so to live that when old age comes you will be spared
the tortures of remorse and regret. It is *not* the correct thing to let your hosts at dinner see that you have
only come for the food; to put on evening dress before
six in the evening; to come down to breakfast in all
your jewels, stars, or orders; for a lady to dance two
successive dances with the same partner, unless she is
engaged to marry him (*O tempora, O mores!*); for
a lady at a dance to go down to supper alone; "she
has to wait upon the kindness of her gentlemen friends
in these matters, unless she is a belle." Mysterious
exception! Used Victorian belles, then, to have the
right of solitary entry to the supper-room? And who

decided which ladies had the necessary qualifications for such lone gourmandising? Would a waiter accost them while they ate their mayonnaise, with "Excuse me, madam, I fear you are not quite up to our standard. Perhaps one of the gentlemen would attend on you . . ."?

Well, it is idle to speculate on the manners of another age. For myself, I have found but little social guidance even in up-to-date works on etiquette. For they never tell you the things you really want to know. I do not want to know how to eat asparagus, nor how to order at a restaurant (order what you want, seems to me the only answer, and no book can tell you what that is), nor how to greet acquaintances in the street. All these seem simple matters. But life is, nevertheless, beset with social problems, to which insufficient attention is paid. One day I shall write a little book of conduct myself, and I shall call it *Social Problems of the Unsociable*. And the root problem, beneath a hundred varying manifestations, is How to Escape. How to escape, that is, at those times, be they few or frequent, when you want to keep yourself to yourself. "Come and see me," we say to each other. "Come and stay. Come and have tea, lunch, dinner, anything." We are so kind and so sociable. We all do it. I too say, "Come and eat with me, stay with me, anything." I have heard of one, driven beyond breeding and manners by such requests, who broke out loudly at an evening party, "No, I'm damned if I do. Why should I?" and then was overcome by shame and remorse for his

gaucherie, and returned stumblingly to the usual course
—"Monday? No, I'm afraid I'm engaged. Tuesday—let me see, I have a feeling there's something else
on on Tuesday . . ." attempting thus to cover up his
disgraceful outbreak. Another I heard of who, pestered with requests that he should do this and that,
stay here and lecture there, attend this meeting or
public dinner, that odious function or bazaar, caused
to be inserted in the *Times* an obituary notice of himself, with "No Flowers." But, alas! his last state was
worse than his first, for, though flowers did not come,
letters of condolence and cards of kind inquiry (as if,
forsooth, when a man's dead there is anything left to
inquire about) poured in upon his angry relatives, until they, able to endure it no more, inserted in the
*Times* a notice saying that Mr. So-and-So had recov-
ered after all. No; death, unless strictly genuine, is no
way out.

What solution, then, does life offer? There are two
obvious courses: you may do the things suggested, at
infinite tedium to yourself; or you may be rude. Both
these courses are crude, and unworthy of a subtle brain.
A third course is to have a card printed with "Miss
Blank, or Mr. Dash, is unable to fulfil any engage-
ments at present, owing to pressure of business, of
family affairs, health, recent bereavement, and an im-
minent journey round the world." (Give them the
lot, and let them take their pick.) But this will only
serve for postal communications, and does not solve the
problem of invitations by word of mouth. The only

solution of these is the Lie Direct. If it is a sin, let it be on the heads of those who tempt you.

I seem to be writing as if all invitations were to be evaded, as if there was never any social act in which one liked to participate. This, of course, is not the case. But invitations one desires to accept present no problem. All one has to do is to throw over one's other obligations, whether of business or pleasure, and accept them. According to the books on etiquette, it is then that the social problems arise. At the dinner-table, for instance—how many of the fingers should be simultaneously dabbled in the finger-bowl? What a strain dinner must be to these inquirers! Not that dinner-parties are without their problems. Mainly the problems belong to the hostess. The chief dinner-party problems are two—what to provide to be eaten, and whom to ask to eat it. If, for instance, you desire to have at your table one of a married couple, and not the other, how to proceed? This is a very frequent problem. The wife may be attractive and not the husband, or the other way round. Suppose, for a moment, that it *is* the other way round (and it quite often is, for interesting men marry dull women more frequently than interesting women, who have more distaste for being bored, marry dull men). Supposing, then, that the husband is a desirable asset at a dinner-party and the wife not—how should the hosts act? There are many solutions open. You may ask both together, and endure the wife; this is the usual pro-

cedure, but a bore. You may ask neither, and have a
duller man instead of the husband; but this is a pity.
You may ask the husband and say, "Leave your wife
at home, for she is tedious"; but this is rude. You
may, after having asked both, cause to be dispatched
to the wife shortly before the party a decoy telegram
from some likely place, saying, "Coming at once, your
mother (or other relative known to exist) dying"; but
this costs a shilling. You may, instead, offer cocktails
to your guests as they arrive and cause the cocktail
of the wife to be drugged, so that the wife, having
partaken, slumbers so heavily as to require to lie down
upstairs all the evening; but this is risky, as people re-
act very differently to drugs, and some are sick. Other
methods will occur readily to any proficient hostess,
and need not here be described at length.

The life of the hostess is, of course, full of problems;
they are far greater than those of the guest. Supposing that you have people staying in your house.
The main problem then is, how to cause them to leave
it as speedily as may be. A branch problem is, what
to do with them while they remain, that they may give
you as little trouble as possible. You should arrange
expeditions for them, to some place of pleasure or interest in the neighbourhood, and then at the last moment back out yourself, on the grounds of household
cares, a headache, or what not. On no account must
they be allowed to say that they will, in that case, stay
at home too. They must go out and stay out, until
the hour appointed by you for them to return. They

must not be permitted to hang about the house while you get on with your avocations.

As to the guests, their problem is how to get away before the date arranged for the termination of their visit. Telegrams, self-sent, are often useful here. While they yet remain, their problem is how to be as little bored as possible, and how to arrange their own days in their own way, if possible going out by themselves and leaving their hosts at home. With hearts of both guests and hosts thus set upon a single aim, one would imagine it easily arranged; but experience shows that it is not so. Politeness steps in, making both parties protest that they desire to devote the day to social intercourse; the hosts entertain, the guests submit to being entertained, and so you get that strange function, a Visit.

You see that I am right in saying that the real social problems are seldom touched on in books. My own book on the subject will, I hope, meet a wide demand.

# PROBLEMS OF MARRIED LIFE

HOW very right and proper it is that the unmarried should be asked to write about the problems of married life! Obviously they should be able to view the matter from a more intelligent and detached standpoint than can the married, and certainly should feel even more free to express themselves upon it. Yet (no doubt because the great majority of adult humanity is married) it has as a rule been the married who have discussed and written about married life. And, according to them, the great and well-nigh insoluble problem is how to be reasonably happy with the partner of your choice. The unmarried may be inclined to say, Why choose a partner with whom happiness is such a dubious achievement? Why not select one approximately suited to your requirements, or go without altogether, which seems simple? There are several answers to this. One is that happiness is a dubious achievement in all circumstances; no state of life, no companionship, is a certain winner in this odd game. Another is that many people agree with Robert Louis Stevenson, that "marriage is terrifying, but so is a cold and forlorn old age," or with Mr. Bernard Shaw that "it is a mistake to get married, but a much bigger mistake not to." A third is that the choice of partner is often made in circumstances of unbalanced emotion hardly compatible with a reasoned judgment; a fourth that no one is really suited to anyone else's requirements, for man will always require more than he can possibly receive. Also man, though infinitely gregarious, is at the same time infinitely solitary. To live, day in, night out, with another human being, whose personality makes perpetual demands upon your own, to practise continual forbearance towards the peccadilloes of one not yourself, to be deprived without term of your individual and sacred liberty, to be trenched upon, hemmed about, and kept in on every side—who is sufficient for these things? To be with the beloved just enough—that is passionately moving and contenting (though you will never know that it is enough). To be with the beloved insufficiently—that is annihilating anguish of soul. To be with the beloved too much— that is surfeit and thraldom. So, anyhow, say those who write on this great theme, though those who live it seem often to survive unstifled and unthralled.

But those who write about it have often more of imagination than of that accuracy of mind necessary for the fair discussion of a subject. They are creative artists, and invent. Take, for instance, Mr. Arnold Bennett. In a recent book, entitled *Our Women,* he discusses the incompatibility of husbands and wives, and cites, as an average example of differences between those who love, a quarrel between a husband of ordinarily decent habits and principles and a manifestly vicious, dishonest, and unbalanced wife. His argument is (apparently), men are like this and women are like that; how, then, shall they understand one another and get on? How indeed! We could none of us, certainly, get on with the fearful female he depicts. But morality is not actually and as a point of plain fact as unfairly distributed between the sexes; on the whole the balance, in nearly all the virtues, is pretty even, and you will find about as many women of honest habit and unmalicious temper as men. Of course, if a man chooses to marry a liar and a shrew, he has himself to thank, and he should not have his case cited as an average one, any more than should a woman who does the same thing. They should both have been more careful, and married someone with approximately the same code of ethics and breeding as their own.

Then there is Mr. Wells, who wrote once a very interesting novel called *Marriage,* in which he implied that the trouble often is that the man, an intelligent being, wants to be busy about his life's work, while the woman, acquisitive, monkey-like, and an intellectual and moral imbecile, only wants to spend his money and distract his attention. Again the reply is, do not marry intellectual and moral imbeciles of either sex. It is really so easy not to.

There is also Robert Louis Stevenson, who makes the surprising statement that boys and girls are taught different codes of morality. This may (possibly, but improbably) have been so in his days, but it is certainly not so now. People are indeed taught different codes of morality, but according to class, parentage, race, and environment, not according to sex. You do not hear parents saying to their little boys, "Little girls may get angry and hit, but you may not," or to their small daughters, "Little boys may steal, but not little girls."

Then there is Mr. Galsworthy, from whom one might infer that the trouble often is that the husband is a sensual and callous brute. The same answer holds —those women who marry such cannot be called average cases; and anyhow, if they do not find their husbands out before matrimony, they are probably pretty callous and sensual themselves, so ought to get on all right.

However, granted that one of these sad mistakes has been made, and so rash a marriage perpetrated— given that a man or woman has contracted to live with another to whom he or she is unsuited, intellectually, physically, or morally, it is, no doubt, a bad business, and may become, if sufficiently thought about, a problem, to which there would appear to be only three profitable solutions. You may end the sad affair at once; you may Coué it into tolerable form by repeating "Day by day and in every way we get on better and better"; or you may set your teeth and bear it, seeking such alleviations as may be found elsewhere, which is the course normally adopted.

But there are, of course, problems in married life, as in all life, even when such profound incompatibility of temper and habit is not one of them. You will find them, these problems, set forth in some of those bright and touching columns of chat which adorn the Woman's Page, so called, of much of our daily and weekly press. You do not find them so often on the Pages for Men. Perhaps men are less interested in such problems, or perhaps can more readily solve them for themselves. Anyhow, those authorities who decide what shall interest woman to read have arranged that she shall be offered (in addition to advice on toilet soaps, cosmetics, garments, and ways of dealing with children and food) hints on how to conduct her court-ship and marriage. These hints are, so far as I have observed, based on the assumption that to keep her husband's regard will be a strenuous and unceasing struggle; she must use very device to retain it, or it will slip from her. She must look fresh, bright, and pretty in the evenings, to welcome her husband on his return from work. (What she is to do if her husband does his work at home we are not told; prob-ably it is a bad business.) She must see that the house is tidy, the food succulent ("tasty" is the Woman's Page word); in short, she must be a bright little wifie in a cosy little home. Should she have a hole in her stocking or an unbecoming dress, should the bacon be burnt or the sago too frequent—hey, presto! love will fly. All this must be very alarming to young wives, and must make life appear a battle-field indeed. The husband, on the other hand, may, one infers, appear sometimes with a button missing, or inadequately shaved, without incurring the loss of his wife's regard; nor will inferior food shatter her love. A wife's affection is regarded by these helpful writers as a far more stable business than that of a husband, which would seem to be for ever straining at the cable.

But the husband too has, doubtless, his problems and difficulties. To live with a woman and children is a curious life for a man of affairs to choose. Perhaps the lesser animals manage better. To come home from work every evening to this old *ménage,* this strange assortment of fellow-creatures, so near to, and yet so far from, oneself, to find one's house alive and noisy with the rudimentary human beings whom one has produced, only partially kept in order by that only slightly less rudimentary human being with whom one has elected to pass one's life—this is indeed a queer adventure.

Personally, were I a husband, which I see small chance of ever being, I should not greatly care about it. I should wish the adventure never undertaken, the too enterprising past undone, and myself a free man once more. Indeed, many a husband does frequently wish this. But some bear it with surprising equanimity. After all, they, too, are rudimentary creatures, and what better of life have they a right to expect? What better, they presumably reflect, can they do than to assist in that great human enterprise of peopling the already over-peopled earth with others of their kind? And many men rather like a woman about the home; what with one thing, what with another, she has her uses.

But there is, there must be, for both husband and

wife the problem (unless they fail to recognise it, in which case it cannot, presumably, be called a problem) of how to avoid the weariness that comes from monotony. "One cannot eat always of the same dish," say the truthful natives of a Central African tribe; be that as it may, they make no attempt to do so. These unsophisticated brethren of ours, who face life's problems with so cheerful and so manly a simplicity, have some curious and happy devices to avoid connubial weariness, many of which are recounted by Professor Westermarck in his immense and erudite *History of Human Marriage*. Some tribes make an interchange of partner a regular feature of a visit to friends. What an interest must a week-end visit among these cheery people be to all the four concerned! Others change partners at the new moon; others, again, have such a variety of wives that it is not necessary to change them at all—until, of course, they have lost their attractions.

But such devices for happier marriage are not smiled on by Western custom or law. We may desire to change our husbands or our wives, but so troublesome is the enterprise made that most people are content to acquiesce in the state to which they have called themselves, and face, cheerfully or otherwise, the problems of a monotonous monogamy. It is very probable, of course, that polygamy too has its personal problems, no less acute, and more in number. Indeed, no condition of being, however married, however single, is safeguarded from these. And the retention of mutual regard is by no means necessarily the acutest of them. Unless you belong to the Constructive Birth Control Society (which professes to regulate the supply of infants, and to make the world safe from babies), children will arrive. The chief problem of married life is then how to dispose of what Mr. Bernard Shaw has aptly called these predatory little creatures, so as to occasion the minimum of disturbance and inconvenience in the home. Those with large enough houses can keep the nursery and its denizens at sufficient distance from the rest of the house to muffle the wild-beast sounds which will proceed therefrom. Those with small space at their command, and not enough money to keep employees who will cope with the matter, must manage as best they can. As the infants emerge from the merely menagerie stage and get a little older, the problem will be how to make them at once happy and good; and one may as well admit at once that it is insoluble. No one is both happy and good; the two qualities are, indeed, incompatible: you have to take your choice, and lucky is he who gets either. Parents have to choose for their young. They must either give the children their way and encourage them to be nuisances to their neighbours and indulgent to their own appetites and whims (in which case the infants will suffer severe and prolonged disappointment in later life, on finding it so inferior to its bright beginnings); or they must check, curb, tame, and subdue the little creatures—in fine, make them sad, but approximately virtuous (they will then

enjoy their grown-up life more, by contrast with its
dark approach). Either method is a great source of
trouble to the parents: for if they adopt the former they
will be continually pestered and disturbed by the follies,
riots, orgies, and consequent sicknesses they have not
checked, and if they choose the latter they will be for
ever called upon to vociferate displeasure and apply
discipline. It is, altogether, an unfortunate business,
this of bringing up and being brought up. These
strange little savages that we all are, without virtue
or learning, flung into a world that has to accept us
and drag us somehow through our more depraved and
foolish years, find replies to our imbecile sayings, keep
us under, and yet not crush us! A strange business,
and not, as a rule, at all well done. Yet it must be
done somehow; for if these little creatures were not
allowed to survive there would be no grown-up people,
and that would, some day, be a calamity, though others
may think that that is as may be.

On the whole, and taking them all round, it seems
probable that the problems of married life are over-
regarded by theorists and writers, and insufficiently
by prospective marriers. If the latter class thought
more about them, the former would have the less to
say. However, one may sum up in the words of Mr.
Bernard Shaw's wise greengrocer: "Marriage is tolerable enough in its way, if you're easy-going and don't
expect too much from it. But it doesn't bear thinking
about. The great thing is to get the young people tied
up before they know what they're letting themselves
in for."

# PROBLEMS OF A WOMAN'S LIFE

LIFE—any life—is full of problems. Already I have considered many of them. Let us now think of the problems appertaining in particular to women. There is no reason why one should not, if one likes, separate and consider some of the problems incidental to belonging, as we nearly all must, to one of the two sexes commonly found upon this planet. There are such problems, though most problems have a wider application and present themselves impartially to those of both sexes. But not all. There are occasions when a problem arises for a woman merely because she is a woman. Such, for instance, as shingling the hair.

Let us consider, for example, jurywomen. The learned judge is apt to turn kindly to the honest twelve and remark, "There are some (or there is one) unmarried women in the jury. They (or she) may retire before the hearing of this case." (There are also, probably, some unmarried men among the jury, but judges do not seem to think that these have minds capable of tarnish from anything they may hear. It is, for some odd reason, only women whom marriage is supposed to harden from sensitiveness to insensibility. Men are not thus affected, possibly they were hardened before.) So here is the problem. Is the unmarried jurywoman to retire at the judge's word, like a child ordered out of the room before a private conversation, and look a fool? Or is she to stay where she is, and be thought a hardened, insensible, and unwomanly creature? Or is she to raise a question about what marriage has to do with it and why marriage affects only one sex, and be thought insubordinate and over-inquiring? Or is she to depart, but with an explanation, remarking that she does not in the least object to hearing anything, but that she has business elsewhere and would rather attend to it, and be thought unworthy of the rights of a citizen? Or is she to pretend not to hear, and be thought deaf or half-witted? I offer no solution: I merely state the problem.

More serious and more frequent in the normal feminine life is the problem of what is called house-keeping. Minding the home. Running the house. This strange occupation has many names, but they all mean the same thing. Ordering meals. Telling the cook what to prepare; or, rather, being told by the cook what she intends to prepare. To those who do not housekeep, it seems as if this conversation with the cook was a trifle unnecessary. Be sure that the cook will prepare something to eat; it is her job, and you had much better leave her to it, instead of worrying her with ignorant suggestions or protests or idle chit-chat. "That will do very nicely," I have heard many of such dialogues end. Well, then, if it will do very nicely, why talk about it beforehand?

For God's sake, let the cook cook, the housemaid house-maid, the laundress launder, the dustman remove his dust, without interference. There is no reason why all this interference should be one of the problems of a woman's life. Further, if someone has got to house-keep, there is no reason why it should be a woman rather than a man. But that is the convention.

Often—alas! too often—there are no servants. Then someone, of one sex or another, it does not matter which, has got to do something about it. Men have proved themselves far cleverer than women in shelving this onerous duty. A tradition has now for long been established that cooking and cleaning are woman's work. As these occupations are among the most tiresome which humanity has to endure, this tradition is very unfortunate for women. But there it is; and the problem is how to get what is needful done as rapidly as possible, so that one can go and do something else, more lucrative, interesting, or amusing. There must be something to eat at stated intervals, and the house or the flat must be about as clean as the houses and flats of one's acquaintances. (This is not to say much, since no house or flat is ever very clean.)

It sounds simple, but actually to secure both these results will often be found to take the entire time. All the time there is. And that is so tragically little. None left over for reading, writing, walking, sitting in woods, playing games, making love, merely existing without effort. And ever at your back you hear Time's winged chariot hurrying near . . . and so the grave yawns, and at the end you will be able to say, not "I have warmed both hands before the fire of life," but "I have Kept House."

The only solution of this problem which I can suggest—and I almost hesitate to do so—is, Do *not* keep house. Let the house, or flat, go unkept. Let it go to the devil, and see what happens when it has gone there. At the worst, a house unkept cannot be so distressing as a life unlived.

What is commonly supposed to be another problem specifically feminine is that of Beauty, how to acquire it, or how to retain it when any. Mrs. Atherton, in a recent and rather entertaining novel, suggests one solution of this problem. Her heroine, at the age of sixty, has her ductless glands X-rayed, and is restored thereby to her marvellous beauty and youth of thirty years before. Here is indeed a solution of one of the most acute of female problems. Other solutions will be found (I expect) among the advertisement columns of any magazine for ladies. For myself I have no remedy to offer for this distressing and almost universal complaint of Losing the Looks—except, grin and bear it. Consider also that men, too, suffer from it (though apparently less acutely), that life is at best a brief and perishing episode, that in the grave none are beautiful, and that anyhow human beauty is an artificial convention, varying from period to period of history, and from country to country. In certain parts of the globe blubber lips, flat noses, and woolly hair are all the rage. Who knows, then, but that at any moment withered faces or double chins may not come in? There is hope for all, and none need despair; and beauty, anyhow, is but skin deep. And so on and so forth; similar maxims of consolation will occur to all. Let us leave the subject and consider sartorial problems —those of them which belong peculiarly to women. The chief of these is, of course, how to dress well on expenditure insufficient for that purpose. And it may at once be admitted that this is impossible. You must either dress badly or spend more money than you wish to—in most cases more than you have got. It is a simple alternative, and every woman must make up her own mind which she intends to adopt. Many woman adopt both. Another sartorial problem has always been how to reconcile a certain conformity to fashion with a certain comfort and grace. This problem is not so acute just now as it has often been in the past—in the days, for instance, of crinolines, bustles, tight waists, hobble skirts, long trains, and the other monstrosities of fashion which have come and gone. But it is always there; and if long skirts—that most clumsy and unlovely of fashions—come in again, it will become acute. And it, too, is insoluble. You cannot be at once graceful, comfortable, and in the mode. Probably you will be none of these things. Life is hard for women, as the saying goes.

One article is not enough in which to consider feminine problems at large. Turn the pages of a female magazine, and problems of which you had not thought confront you on every page. How to clean chintzes.

Yes, indeed. Why look lined and unlovely? Is your neck too fat? Is it too thin? How to prepare hearty meals of eggs. How to express your personality by your scent; how to perfume the ears. Are you nearly bald? How to dress the kiddies, keep the home nice, make your husband comfortable, succeed in business or at the Bar, use your vote, choose a car . . . What a life is this into which we have been flung!

But it should console women to consider that, as a sex, they have fewer problems than they had some forty or fifty years ago. Not long since I was reading an *Observer* of the eighteen-nineties, and there was a leading article on the habits of the modern young woman, among which was mentioned with contumely the growing custom of demanding latch-keys to the front door of their homes. No explanation is given as to why this simple and labour-saving device is reprehensible for the feminine sex. But, if it was really unusual, life must have held for women a problem we do not have now—how to get in to their own houses without continually disturbing the maids at their work. In those far days the whole of life must have been, for women, a problem indeed. They could not so much as ride on a bicycle or in a hansom cab without a chorus of voices denouncing them as "fast." Women were the world's butts; Aunt Sallies put up for shies. The problem was, no doubt, how to have your good time in spite of this. Many of our ancestresses achieved it, but against what odds! We are, there is no doubt about it, happier to-day.

THE END